# REBOUND RULES

## *Also by Rick Pitino*

Born to Coach

Full-Court Pressure

Success Is a Choice

Lead to Succeed

# RICK PITINO

*with PAT FORDE*

# REBOUND RULES

## The Art of Success 2.0

**COLLINS**

*An Imprint of HarperCollins Publishers*

HarperCollins books may be purchased for educational, business, or sales promotional use. For information, please write: Special Markets Department, HarperCollins Publishers, 10 East 53rd Street, New York, NY 10022.

FIRST EDITION

Library of Congress Cataloging-in-Publication Data

Pitino, Rick.
    Rebound rules : the art of success 2.0 / Rick Pitino with Pat Forde.—1st ed.
        p. cm.
    Includes index.
    ISBN 978-0-06-162663-0
 1. Pitino, Rick.   2. Basketball coaches—United States—Biography.   3. Basketball—Coaching—United States.   4. Success.   I. Forde, Pat, 1964–   II. Title.

    GV884.P57A3   2008
    796.323092—dc22
    [B]                                                          2008028622

08   09   10   11   12   WBC/RRD   10   9   8   7   6   5   4   3   2   1

To all the children of September 11, a senseless tragedy, my thoughts and prayers are with you. May God bless your lives.

# *Acknowledgments*

Thank you to Boston University, Providence College, the New York Knicks, the University of Kentucky, the Boston Celtics, and the University of Louisville for this special opportunity.

—Rick Pitino

Thanks to Rick Pitino for bringing as much passion, hunger, and drive to this collaboration as he does to coaching basketball—it was an amazing experience. Thanks to my bosses at ESPN.com for the occasional slices of spare time to complete this project—your understanding is greatly appreciated. And thanks to Tricia, Mitchell, Clayton, and Brooke Forde for their support, encouragement, understanding, and general good cheer—you are my inspiration.

—Pat Forde

# Contents

# Anatomy of a Comeback

**W**ITH 15:30 TO PLAY ON Fat Tuesday night in Baton Rouge in 1994, my University of Kentucky basketball team was getting killed. We trailed Louisiana State 68–37. If you asked anyone in the Pete Maravich Assembly Center at that moment, the game was over.

Anyone that is but the guys in the blue uniforms.

Against all odds, we kept believing that we had a chance and kept playing. Why? Because we had an enormous amount of pride and self-esteem—and a little arrogance as well. We were accustomed to winning, and imposing our will on opponents. Nobody treated us the way LSU had treated us, and we were determined to do something about it. Still, we had to stay in touch with our fundamentals and make this comeback in small steps.

If I had called everyone into the huddle with 15 minutes left and said, "We're definitely going to win," that would have been false bravado and the players would have seen through it. One thing you must do in the face of adversity is to be honest with yourself, and with the people you're trying to lead. Acknowledge the difficult spot you're in and commence digging out of it. Don't point fingers, don't recriminate, and don't make excuses. Stay positive and get to work.

So the first thing we had to do was salvage our dignity over the next few minutes—to simply stop the bleeding and start making a small dent in that deficit. Down 31, the grand scheme at that very moment wasn't to emerge with a victory at night's end; looking that far ahead would have blurred our focus on the gradual progress that comprises every comeback. The goal was to get within 20 points as quickly as possible. To do that, we concentrated on three things: using our press to create turnovers, fouling the two shaky free throw shooters LSU had on the floor, and getting high-percentage shots.

All three worked, and the turnaround actually happened faster than expected. In about five minutes of clock time, we'd shockingly chopped the deficit from 31 to 14. Our frantic style of play helped—speeding up the game and increasing the possessions for both teams gave us more chances to rally. Stubbornly, we kept whittling away at LSU's lead, as the celebrating crowd turned more and more nervous. Every timeout Tigers' coach Dale Brown called in an attempt to slow our momentum actually raised our spirits. We knew we had them rattled; we knew we had a chance.

We had little-used reserves making shots, stealing passes, and grabbing rebounds. Finally, Walter McCarty dropped in a three-point shot with 19 seconds left and we took the lead, 96–95, and went on to win 99–95. To this day, it remains the biggest comeback in college basketball history on the road. The game quickly became known nationwide as the Mardi Gras Miracle. It was certainly memorable, but it was no miracle. It didn't take divine intervention to win that game; it took an unbreakable optimism, and a plan for coming back.

I've been a part of other great rallies: When I coached the New York Knicks in the 1980s, we came from 27 points down to beat Portland; in 1995 my Kentucky team trailed defending national champion Arkansas by six points with 38 seconds left in overtime in the Southeastern Conference tournament championship and won; we rallied from 10 down in the final minute to beat Tennessee my first year at Louisville; and in 2005 we trailed West Virginia by 20 points in an NCAA tournament regional final game and won to reach the Final Four.

Here is the important common denominator in all those comebacks: They began with positive energy on the floor, on the bench, and in the team huddles.

They began with a belief that things would get better if we persevered through adversity, trusted each other and worked together. They began with a conviction that consistent effort, even against long odds, inevitably would turn the tide. They began with a reliance on the fundamentals that made us a successful team to begin with, and we didn't desert them in a crisis. They began with a single good play, and a certainty that one good play would lead to another and another and another until the deficit was gone and the game was won.

The most important thing I did in the course of those comebacks was to build my players' self-esteem. Don't tear them down for the mistakes that got the team in those holes to begin with; build them up to the point where they felt capable of making the plays that would result in victory.

When people feel extraordinary, you get extraordinary results. When people feel ordinary, you get ordinary results. I'm not talking about false patronage; don't tell little Johnny he's going to be president when he's not doing well in the classroom. They have to deserve it—and when they do deserve it, you have to reinforce it in stressful times.

There have been times when I've not been as positive with my teams during games. I have succumbed to the frustration of the moment and filled the huddle with negative energy, telling them, "This is what you deserve because you practiced poorly." There certainly is a time for constructive criticism and even an outright tail chewing, but it's generally not when you're trying to rally people to redouble their efforts and perform at a higher level. That deprives your team of the hope that it can come back in adverse situations.

When it comes to team dynamics—on a basketball court or in a corporate setting—maintaining a positive atmosphere is crucial. The most positive basketball team I've been around was in the 1986–87 season at Providence College. We played an excellent Georgetown team four times that season. We won the first game at home—a game where I almost got into a heated verbal altercation on the sidelines with the great coach of the Hoyas, John Thompson. Afterward Big John, a glowering, six-foot-ten Providence alum, draped an arm around my shoulders and said, "I'm proud of what you're doing with my alma mater. But when you come to D.C., we're going to kick your ass."

Big John was true to his word. His team not only killed us at home, but did it again in the Big East Conference tournament. After that game, I tried to stay as positive as possible with our team going into Selection Sunday, when the NCAA tournament bracket is unveiled. I told my players, "Let's enjoy this experience, work hard, and see what we accomplish. The only team that has our number is Georgetown, and we won't see them again."

Sure enough, the bracket was released and we were in the same region as Georgetown. If both of us won our first three games, we'd meet in the regional final for the chance to go to the Final Four. Still, that seemed like a long shot for us. But lo and behold, we won our first three games and squared off with the Hoyas for a fourth time. Before that game, I poured on the positive energy. I told our players, "In every great achievement, you need some luck. And you guys are the luckiest bunch I've ever seen. The one thing you'd want is to play a team that will take you lightly, and that's Georgetown. You have the biggest psychological advantage of all time."

We also went to work tactically for that game, completely changing our offense from shooting three-pointers on the perimeter to attacking the basket. It worked. We shocked the Hoyas and won easily, advancing to the Final Four to highlight a fairy-tale season.

Current University of Florida coach Billy Donovan was the best player on that Providence College team. Years later, Billy asked me whether I really believed that pep talk about how lucky the team was to draw Georgetown again. "Absolutely not," I told him, laughing, but when you're trying to overcome an obstacle, sometimes that's what it takes. Being relentlessly positive can be the only way to come back and defeat towering negativity.

In recent years, I've had to apply those same comeback fundamentals to adversities greater than anything encountered in a single basketball game. In about eight months, from January 8 to September 11, 2001, I was hit with a series of setbacks far more difficult to overcome than a 31-point deficit in Baton Rouge. During that time I resigned as coach of the Boston Celtics—my first professional failure—and then I lost two brothers-in-law to sudden death in New York City. One was hit by a taxi, and the other, my dearest friend, was killed in the 9/11 attack on the World Trade Center. This combination of events left me with some questions to answer and choices to make: After so many years of success, would I let that failure with the Celtics define me? Or would I learn from it and become a better coach? Would I stew in bitterness over the senseless deaths of Don Vogt and Billy Minardi? Or would I gain a new perspective and appreciation for life?

I had to make a two-pronged comeback: one in my professional life and one in my personal life. Chances are good that at some point in time, you'll have to do the same. Nobody goes through life without setbacks and struggles, some of them significant enough to cause you to doubt everything you believe in. You might be fired. You might face serious illness for you or your family. You might have a major financial setback, face an ethical dilemma, or find yourself starting over later in life. You might see a lifetime goal disintegrate, leaving you in a place you never imagined when plotting out your career path.

Will you have a gameplan in place to make your comeback? You should, because the comeback is a classic American trait: We are a second-chance people. The story of the United States was not written by people who were handed everything. It was written by people reinventing their lives after encountering adversity—by immigrants and cast-offs from foreign lands who took a leap of faith to make a new start in a new land.

After my job ended with the Celtics, I had to pull myself out of a crater by rediscovering what I call my PHD—my passion, my hunger, and my drive. I had to quit beating up on myself and elevate the self-esteem that I always have tried to keep so high in my players. It was time for me to coach myself.

It took weeks of reflection, but I eventually got through to myself. When I decided to return to college coaching and got my current job at Louisville, I had repaired and prepared my psyche. I was ready to make a comeback—but the tragic deaths provided another hurdle in the midst of making that comeback. This time I had to think more than usual about other people—how to help my family deal with these losses and how to help those who had lost a husband and a father. I had to step outside myself.

As difficult as it was going through those things, I've emerged as a wiser and happier person. I wouldn't wish some of those moments on anyone, but they've been learning experiences that will shape the later stages of my career and my life after basketball. My perspective now is totally different. Basketball is my passion, but not my life. Helping my players, family members, and friends achieve happiness counts more than the final score of any game. I'm still enjoying what I do immensely and my energy to work remains extremely high—but there is a greater balance at the end of the day.

There are plenty of books about succeeding in life and in business, but there aren't a lot of books that tell you how to prepare and execute a different strategy if your original path doesn't lead to the end of the rainbow. *Rebound Rules* will help you make your own comeback. It delves into the insidious nature of self-doubt, and tells you how to combat it by facing your fears and failures and learning from them. It explores the emotional trauma of tragedy, how it can affect your life, and how you can eventually overcome it and gain a new perspective. It details the personal fundamentals that can be relied upon daily to help you get through those difficult times. It examines the painstaking rally we must make to achieve greatness without shortcuts; living the "practice-makes-perfect" credo. It discloses the dangers inherent once greatness is achieved—complacency, grandiosity, and a blurred focus—and how to combat them. It explains the poise and confidence needed to keep your long-range goals intact in an accelerated world, where impatient pursuit of a quick fix can turn temporary setbacks into major setbacks.

This book proposes how to turn new challenges into new methods of success, while also improving our old methods. It shows the necessity of identifying great talent, surrounding yourself with it, fostering its growth, and using it as a support system in tough times. It probes the formula for great chemistry within an organization—and finds ways to prevent a rogue element from ruining that chemistry. It promotes a different means for calculating your net worth—your net worth to others, that is, not to your company's bottom line. It presents a means for rejuvenating yourself on the cusp of retirement by finding a fresh set of challenges to undertake. And once you reached a career's end, having survived all the ups and downs that can be encountered in a life's work, it provides a game plan for your final act, how to make it your greatest act yet.

Being confronted with adversity—in sports, in business, in any walk of life—can happen more often than anyone wants to admit. It will test you in ways most of us have never contemplated. Having a plan to deal with it can make your comeback a great one.

# REBOUND
# RULES

# Chapter One

# The Darkness of Doubt

**O**N THE EVE OF MY last game as coach of the Boston Celtics, I sat by the pool at my south Florida vacation home on a spectacular January night in 2001 with my friend and assistant, Jim O'Brien. We were drinking a beer and I was telling "Obie" that this was it. I was quitting tomorrow, after we played the Miami Heat. I was done. He tried to talk me out of it, but there was no way. We were besieged by criticism and negativity in Boston, but it was worst inside my head. It was time to walk away and regroup from my first professional failure.

I already had talked to two of my closest advisers: C. M. Newton, my former boss at the University of Kentucky; and Dave Gavitt, who had served as the commissioner of the Big East Conference during my days coaching at Providence. C. M. advised me to ride out the season and see if it turned around. Dave counseled me to leave now if I really wanted to return to college coaching in the spring.

It was with this counsel in mind that I told Obie my plan that night by the pool. When the team flies back to Boston, I told him, I was going to stay in Miami and he would take over as interim head coach. I'm an old-school guy whose response to difficult circumstances has always been to regroup and try harder—but simply trying hard wasn't going to fix this situation. We had won 12 games and lost 21 to that point, and this was our fourth straight season with a losing record. Defeat had beaten me down. "I love this game," I said. "But for the past year and a half, I haven't enjoyed one practice or one game. You're going to be the coach. It's a beginning for you. It's an end for me." Obie looked up at the full moon, looked around at the beautiful surroundings, and smiled. "It's not a bad life, man."

He was right, of course. There are many worse things in life than resigning from a multimillion-dollar job and spending the rest of the winter in a beautiful home and beautiful weather—but the truth is, my life was pretty bad on the inside at that moment. The old adage about money not buying happiness was never truer than right then. I believe if you chase money, you're not necessarily chasing success. Give yourself success, and money will chase after you as if it's your shadow.

I had chased the biggest contract in basketball history to Boston: 10 years, $50 million. I had made the move for the money. I was ready to admit my high-stakes mistake and quit.

It's hard to articulate the disappointment I felt. I had left a dream job at the University of Kentucky after going to three Final Fours, winning the 1996 national championship, and returning a scandal-scarred program to the forefront of college basketball. It had been eight years of good times and great accomplishments. The only thing that could convince me to leave was this chance of a lifetime, to take over the most storied franchise in NBA history. By my game plan, I would take the Celtics from the lowest depths of professional basketball and return it to the glorious heights enjoyed with Auerbach, Russell, Cousy, Havlicek, and Bird—but for the first time as a basketball coach, I hadn't gotten the job done.

There were mitigating factors. Missing out on future Hall of Famer Tim Duncan in the 1997 draft lottery, despite having the worst record the previous year, was just plain bad luck. An owner lockout that shortened the 1998–99 season after we'd made a 21-game improvement the previous year was bad timing. The stabbing of our best player, Paul Pierce, was the worst—he had been jumped in a Boston nightclub by a local rapper's posse and stabbed repeatedly. I was with his mother at his hospital bedside in September 2000, when the doctors told us his attacker missed by a quarter of an inch from dealing Paul a lethal blow. For a while we were simply hoping he'd live, much less play again. Paul made a remarkable comeback that season, but it did not trigger team success.

So as my friend Bill Parcells says, you are your record—and my record in Boston was 102–146. We never made the playoffs. I have never taken losing well, and now it had become my identity: With the Celtics, at least, I was a loser. I was stumbling through the darkness of doubt.

Nobody's professional growth curve is an unbroken upward line. That just doesn't happen, in any career field. Failures will occur. Crises will crop up. Confidence and self-esteem will be challenged, and in such times, people accustomed to success will experience the darkness of doubt, something that can attack you professionally, personally, and spiritually. Every single person will, at one point or another, have this experience. It is darkness. You're afraid—and when fear comes in, you make poor decisions.

I am a positive person by nature, but more by habit. I've worked at it. That outlook has been instrumental to me in motivating young players, rebuilding fallen programs and becoming the only coach in college basketball history to take three different schools to Final Fours—but it doesn't provide a foolproof firewall against insidious doubt. Doubt can spring up from a variety of sources: losing, adversity, financial insecurity, age, illness, injury, family issues, even success. A longtime doctor might be facing a malpractice suit. A lawyer may have made an error that blew a high-profile case. A salesman may lose a big account. I have experienced the darkness of doubt twice professionally. I'll discuss the second time later in this chapter, but the first time already had gripped me as I sat poolside in Miami with Jim O'Brien.

Before that final game against the Heat, I told the players one by one that I was resigning. Walter McCarty, a player I had coached at Kentucky, winning the 1996 national championship, was disappointed. Pierce gave me a hug with tears in his eyes. We lost the game, and afterward I went back to my vacation home alone. I'd left my family back in the Northeast, telling them I needed time—maybe a month—to figure out what to do with my life.

I had never taken time off in my life, and now I had a surplus of it. Free time in January? That was a foreign concept to me; I hadn't experienced it since I was a young child. At first, I didn't use that time constructively. I had given back $23 million in salary by quitting, but it was worth it to escape the ugliness. The booing fans and media rip jobs were unpleasant, but marinating in self-doubt was worse. My normally strong self-esteem cracked. I wrote down every mistake I made on the job: bad personnel moves, bad coaching decisions, bad reactions to adverse situations. I used them all to cudgel myself.

I made three big mistakes with the Celtics. First of all, I made too many spontaneous decisions about players. Patience is a virtue, even in this microwave society, and I churned our roster too quickly by making snap judgments about who could and couldn't help us. As a CEO, you have to give people time to prove themselves, one way or another. Secondly, I was learning that there are no shortcuts. If talent is limited, it's simply going to take a great deal of perseverance and patience to change things. You can't ask for a new hand of cards or to be dealt cards as if they could be dealt you from under the table. You must play the hand you have at the time. Third, the biggest thing I learned is that when failure is in the air, you cannot beat yourself up about it. People who have failed after achieving a certain level of success often go in two mistaken directions: They make excuses for why it's not their fault or they start beating themselves up.

It was in this mental state that I almost found myself in the coaching version of a whirlwind rebound marriage. UNLV, another school with a proud basketball tradition that had fallen on hard times, had fired its coach during the season and was looking to line up a replacement. Within three weeks of leaving the Celtics, they were offering me the job. I admit that it felt great to be wanted again, and I met some great people while taking a look at it. My wife, Joanne, and I had become friends with Las Vegas hotel magnates Steve and Elaine Wynn, and they were lobbying me to take the job. In the end, Joanne and I decided that it wasn't at the right time or in the right place for us. We'd never lived in the West, and more importantly, I hadn't sorted through the Celtics failure well enough to move on. In my current state of mind, I would only have been taking that job to run away from the doubt that had followed me out of Boston. It's best to avoid making major career decisions while in the throes of an existential crisis.

After saying no to UNLV, I got serious about pulling myself

out of the darkness, ridding myself of the doubt. I got an unexpected assist from a new friend and neighbor, a former pop singer named Steve Alaimo. He came from a totally different profession and knew nothing about basketball. He spent his time in south Florida, running a recording studio and a fishing charter, enjoying life. Once upon a time, he was a pretty big deal in the music industry. He was a teen-idol pop singer in the 1960s who owned a record label and hosted a TV show, *Where the Action Is*. He'd toured with James Brown, performed at the Copacabana, and was friends with Connie Francis and Dion and the Belmonts. We'd go to Gulfstream Park to watch the ponies run, then come back to my house for a glass of wine and talk about our lives. I appreciated hearing a fresh perspective. During those discussions, Steve helped me realize: I had to stop trashing myself for the Celtics failure. "Look," he said, "I wish I was still performing at the Copa, but I'm not. You have to move on. You can't spend your time reliving every mistake and every regret." It was what I needed to hear, and it helped to hear it from someone outside of basketball and my family. Gradually I came to realize that I had to create a new philosophy and stir a new passion.

I started working to rejuvenate myself. The final 18 months with the Celtics had been incredibly stressful, mentally and physically. I began to relish the free time and took stock of what I had learned the hard way.

I alone as a basketball coach could not dictate whether we won or lost, just as a CEO cannot alone dictate profit or loss. I began to understand what a team is all about. The old expression says there's no "I" in "team," but a lot of coaches think there is—and they think that they're the "I." That's especially true in college basketball, where player turnover makes the coaches the stars of the show.

When I arrived with the Celtics, I probably had lost a little perspective. The rapid-fire rebuilding jobs at Boston University, Providence, the New York Knicks, and Kentucky had conned me into thinking I could personally overcome the dearth of talent with the Celtics, that it almost didn't matter who the players were, as long as I was coaching them. What I got instead was a great reiteration of that old lesson: Cream rises to the top. We didn't have much cream, and no amount of motivating or strategizing on my part was going to magically change that. After the rock-star treatment I received for eight years at Kentucky, this was a valuable reminder of a coach's place within—and not above—the team dynamic.

After understanding these things, my life received a strong dose of humility. I accepted the fact that if the word "arrogant" had shown up several times in stories written about me, there probably was some truth to it. I owned up to my failures and my flaws—and then I dropped it, as quickly as possible. The realization was added to the wisdom I needed to lead, and it finally gave me a chance to take a clear-eyed look at who I was, where I was, and where I wanted to go. I got reacquainted with my PHD.

Was I still passionate about my chosen career? Absolutely.

Hungry to get back to work? Starving.

Driven to succeed the way I did before the Celtics? Definitely.

All those important fundamental attributes were still there, augmented by a new perspective. Once I got back in touch with my core, I could put Boston behind and start focusing on the next chapter in my career.

Both the Michigan and Louisville jobs were open that spring, and both were potentially great places to work. I took a long look at each, but Joanne and I ultimately decided that the tradition of Louisville and my familiarity with Kentucky would make it the most enjoyable place to be. I took a great deal of heat from Kentucky fans who viewed Louisville as their hated rival and saw me as a traitor for going there, but they didn't understand: This was no betrayal of them, it was simply the best possible reentry point into college basketball for me and my family.

Seven years later, it's still the best place for me. Along the way, we've won an average of 24 games per season, including an unforeseen Final Four run in 2005. In 2008, we made a strong push to the Elite Eight and finished the season ranked in the *USA Today/* ESPN Top 10. We're positioned for success for the foreseeable future. I was able to enjoy that Louisville Final Four team more than my previous visits with Providence in 1987 and Kentucky in 1993, 1996, and 1997, because of the humility I gained after Boston.

However, this wasn't the last time that I'd face professional doubt. It arose again in January 2007, when a promising season seemed to be veering far off track. Fortunately, because of Boston, this time I was able to address it quickly. A crisis that lasted months before was reduced to a matter of hours this time—and I became a better coach because of it. The bus ride from the Joyce Center on the campus of Notre Dame to the South Bend airport is fairly short, but it lasted long enough for me to come face-to-face with deep professional fear that January 3. Our team had just rung in 2007 with a brutal experience. We were thoroughly beaten in our Big East Conference opener by Notre Dame, 78–62, in a game that was not as close as the score. The Fighting Irish were a talented, veteran team and tough to play at home, but watching their players streak through our defense for easy layups and dunks was difficult to take.

Our record was 10–5—not what I had envisioned when we started practice amid widespread October optimism. We were frightfully young, with seven freshmen and sophomores in our primary rotation. We were physically whipped, with three key players all trying to play through significant injuries that limited their effectiveness. And we showed all the warning signs of a team in danger of being swallowed by the brutal Big East competition—again.

The previous season, 2005–06, had been a ten-car pileup of tough circumstances. We had taken a major step up in class from Conference USA, joining a 16-team Big East super conference at a time when we'd just lost the guts of the surprise 2005 Final Four team. We weren't ready to join what many people thought was the toughest league in college basketball history. Combine the vastly increased competition with injuries to some key play- ers, and we struggled to a 21–14 record, missing the NCAA tour- nament. Our fans were deeply disappointed. Making the NIT Final Four was a consolation, setting the stage for what we hoped would be a major rebound season in 2006–07. But now, after being routed by the Fighting Irish, the rebound season was in jeopardy.

As we made that solemn bus ride, I experienced the darkness of doubt again—and this time it wasn't just creeping in. It had barged in and was staring me straight in the face, probably feed- ing on the leftover scars from 2001. There was fear of letting an- other situation spiral out of control.

I had already seen the doubt in the faces of the reporters and broadcasters who covered our team. I had heard it in the voices of fans who'd called my radio show. For the first time, I was being seriously second-guessed in the state of Kentucky. I knew what they were saying around our basketball-crazed town, knew what they were thinking, knew what judgments were being passed: This team doesn't have it. They were ready to give up on an inexperienced and banged-up group of young men, and it was only January. I didn't think that was fair, and despite the early hardships, I had hope that we'd turn the corner by New Year's. Now, however, this blowout at Notre Dame was making me feel the darkness of doubt again.

When the bus arrived at the airport, I told the players to get off first and go through security to wait for our flight. I kept the coaching staff with me. It was time to face this thing head-on. "I'm not sure we're turning this around in the Big East," I told my coaches. "We're not making the necessary progress. We are not getting it done. We'll meet tomorrow and figure out how to remedy this situation."

Before meeting with my staff that Sunday, I went to church at St. Francis of Rome in Louisville and heard Father Jerry Eifler put a name on exactly what I had been experiencing: the darkness of doubt. He used that as a theme in his sermon, and that's where I got the name of this chapter. In church, everyone thinks the sermon is aimed directly at them. I'd never been as sure of that as I was on this January day, when I was facing the fear of failure. Father Jerry's words were spoken to the entire congregation, but they also were spoken to *me*.

While in the seminary, Father Jerry doubted whether he could become a priest because he didn't believe in the immaculate conception. He came across a monk and told him about the darkness of doubt he was enduring. The monk counseled him not to run away from his life's calling because of this momentary darkness—to focus on all his beliefs, and not on this small area of doubt.

It helped me to hear the wisdom of someone who had been

through something that was similar to what I was going through. Both Father Jerry and Steve Alaimo were able to shine some light into my darkness, so I could dissect the doubt and see it for what it was. Seeking the sympathetic shoulder of a coworker, a peer, or a loved one can provide comfort, but wisdom is a greater ally at times like these.

I came out of church knowing that was what I needed to do. I needed to remember what I had going for me and what our team had going for it, and not allow myself to be paralyzed by negatives that did not outweigh the positives. I felt better—but time was of the essence.

We had one week to save our season. It was time to confront our problems and rededicate ourselves to fixing them. It started with a team meeting, which became very emotional. I told the players, "You don't need a coach with this much experience to give this type of performance. It's a waste of your time and my time. If you don't understand what I'm telling you and don't understand what makes a winner, this turnaround isn't possible." They listened soberly. They were surprised at the passion in my voice and the conviction. They didn't realize we were at a crossroads; it was our job to make everyone understand the urgency and change their mindset.

After the group meeting, it was time to meet with two of our most talented but frustrating young players, Terrence Williams and Edgar Sosa. Williams was a sophomore and Sosa a freshman. They were hard workers with a great love for the game, but they were immature and didn't understand how to make the team better. We'd been banging on both of them all year to trust their teammates, to think of passing before shooting, to let the take-charge moments come to them instead of forcing them. The message wasn't sinking in.

Sosa was told he'd be moved from the distributor's role of point guard to shooting guard—a move that would hurt his considerable pride. Point guards—especially a New York point guard, which Sosa is—are supposed to be the guys in charge on the floor. Edgar liked the attention, prestige, and the control that came with that position. The shooting guard is more of a supporting actor's role, not exactly what he had in mind. Confronted with that, he vowed to become more of a pass-first, shoot-second point guard.

Williams was urged to stop trying to answer critics who said he couldn't shoot the three-pointer. His woeful percentages indicated they were right, so why consistently do the thing you can't do at the expense of your strengths? Like Sosa, Williams was convinced of the need to make everyone else better and quit worrying about his own scoring totals.

Now it was time to confront myself. As with the players, I had to realize that tough times are the best times to get back to the fundamentals of what makes you valuable to an organization. I had to remind myself that I was a hard enough worker and good enough coach to lead this turnaround. The bad ending with the Celtics was not a recurring theme. It was behind me—I could fight through this frustrating period and do this job. From the moment we confronted the darkness of doubt, as a team and as individuals, we began to improve.

I made some changes to our lineup for the next game: Juan Palacios, a six-foot-eight, 250-pound power forward, had been playing with a neck and shoulder injury that prevented him from even lifting his arm over his head—he was useless as a scorer, basically just serving as a screener. We removed him from the starting lineup to go with a healthy team that created a different look. We moved the six-foot-six Williams from his natural wing position to power forward, where his athleticism and quickness made him a matchup problem for bigger players, and his tenacity helped him hold his own defensively and in rebounding. We spaced the floor and went back to pressure defense covering all 94 feet of the court. We had a week to get it right, and the changes were dramatic.

We went on the road one week after the Notre Dame debacle and played like a different team, blowing out South Florida by 26 points. We came home and beat Providence by 15, lost a tough game to a very good Marquette team, then reeled off four straight wins. That included crucial road victories over DePaul and Cincinnati, as we stayed small even after Palacios returned to health. Fortunately, Juan had a great team-first attitude that helped our team chemistry. He never complained about coming off the bench.

After a road loss to Villanova and a home loss to eventual Final Four team Georgetown, we were 16–8, unranked and needed a big push down the stretch. This is where NCAA bids and seedings are won and lost, in the final weeks of a long season. We were on a thin tightrope, with little margin for error and some extremely tough games ahead.

We beat South Florida again, then went on the road to play No. 5 Pittsburgh and No. 13 Marquette. Our team realized the obstacles at hand, but I concentrated on two important factors in motivating them for that two-game road swing. I told the team, "This is like a Christmas gift in February, the opportunity to dazzle the NCAA tournament selection committee and help us get in the tournament. So we absolutely have to execute the game plan without mental lapses to win those games." Our team had been prone to losing concentration at key periods in games—just a possession here or there, and suddenly a potential victory was slipping away. We couldn't afford that against Pitt and Marquette.

Fortunately, we had none of any serious consequence. At Pittsburgh, we passed the ball brilliantly, led wire-to-wire, and pulled off our biggest victory of the season—a 13-point win that was never close. We followed that with a last-second triumph at Marquette, despite trailing most of the second half. Suddenly we looked like NCAA tournament material, winning the final six games of the regular season.

By season's end we were a dangerous team—and also an unselfish one. We won 14 of our final 19 games, finished second in the Big East and earned an NCAA tournament bid. After routing Stanford in the first round, we came within seconds of upsetting a veteran Texas A&M team and advancing to the Sweet Sixteen. We finished 24–10, transforming an underachieving season into a successful one. If it hadn't been for what I learned from my Celtic experience, I would not have handled that season the way I did. If we hadn't faced our darkness of doubt and attacked it, none of that would have been possible. In sports, business or life, tough situations can be the incubator of great turnarounds.

## The Darkness of Doubt

**REBOUND RULES:**

+ **Darkness of doubt happens.** Regardless of your background, your upbringing, your profession, or your potential, almost all of us will encounter failure. It's not something that only happens to one out of every 1,000 people. How you deal with it is what matters.

+ **Get in touch with your fundamentals to combat doubt.** The things that make you special and successful will get you through these dark moments. When you arm yourself with the tools to face doubt, it will shrink in size.

+ **Use past mistakes as learning tools,** not as a cudgel to beat yourself up.

**POINTS OF CAUTION:**

+ **Denial doesn't work.** Avoiding facing your doubt will allow it to linger and fester.

+ **Running away doesn't work either.** One of the Rebound Rules is to avoid rebound marriages, like I considered entering into with UNLV.

+ **Don't isolate yourself.** You're not on an island—there are others who have been through something similar, so seek their counsel. If you choose to isolate yourself, you'll wander in the darkness a long time.

Chapter Two

# *Gaining Perspective*

**O**N A BRIGHT TUESDAY MORNING in Louisville in 2001, I was walking out of the basketball office and heading to the airport. I was catching a flight to Detroit to recruit a player named Brandon Jenkins, who would ultimately become a Cardinal. I was back in the college game for the first time since 1997, and it felt great. The Celtics trauma was receding, and practice with my new team was starting in a month. I was full of enthusiasm, enjoying every day in my new job, rejoicing in this fresh start. As I headed out into the September sunshine, I had no idea that my life had just changed irrevocably.

"Coach," yelled my personal assistant, Jeff Noyes. "You need to come back in here. A plane just went through the World Trade Center." I presumed it was a small plane, misguided, creating an accident. When I got in front of a television and saw the smoke billowing from the tower, I knew it was worse than that—much worse. I knew that my brother-in-law and best friend, Billy Minardi, worked for Cantor Fitzgerald on the 105th floor of the

North Tower. He had just returned back to the office after we spent a week together at Pebble Beach—golfing, relaxing, and laughing as always. Time spent with Billy and his exuberant personality was always fun.

Looking at the TV on 9/11, I could feel the dread in my stomach—a feeling I will never forget. I grew up in New York and knew those buildings. I knew this was bad. I dialed Billy's cell phone and couldn't get through. I kept dialing, again and again. Nothing.

The next few days were a whirlwind tour of Hell. We scoured every list of victims and survivors we could find; checked every website that had information on what had happened; called anyone and everyone we knew who might be able to tell us something. At one point we got false hope—a report that Billy had been injured but was alive. It was wrong. By the end of the week, we realized he was no longer with us.

When that happened, some old wounds were reopened. We were unfortunately well-versed in experiencing senseless tragedy. Just six months earlier, Joanne and I had lost another brother-in-law, Don Vogt, who was struck and killed by a cab in Manhattan. Now losing Billy was devastating. It was like traveling back in time to March of 1987, and another moment of shock and grief that I will never forget.

I was the coach at Providence then, and we were riding the bus back to Rhode Island from New York City. We'd lost in the Big East Conference tournament to Georgetown but had so much to be happy about: The school's first NCAA tournament bid in nine years would be announced that Sunday, and our infant son, Daniel, had just been released from the hospital.

Five months earlier, he'd been born prematurely, weighing only four pounds, and he had serious health issues: He had a hole in his heart and a large space in his palate that made eating difficult. With these health issues, they kept Daniel in a hospital in Boston. Joanne drove 90 minutes each way, every day, spending 12 hours at the hospital and feeding Daniel each day with a special goat's nipple to help avoid the palate problem. The doctors said he needed heart surgery, but they wanted to wait until he reached eight pounds first. Since he was doing well, the doctors released him from the hospital. He could be nurtured back to strength at home, then go back in when he was ready for surgery.

Meanwhile, the doctors told Joanne she needed a break from her near-constant hovering over Daniel. They told her to go to New York for the weekend, leave our four boys with their nanny, and watch my Providence team play in the Big East tourney. She did. We were on our way back from that event, about 2½ hours into a very upbeat ride, when our bus was pulled over by a state trooper. Big East commissioner Dave Gavitt, a former Providence coach, was on the NCAA tournament selection committee, so I figured he was sending advance word on our draw and seeding (this was well before cell phones).

"Who are we playing?" I asked the trooper when he came on the bus. "You need to come with me," he replied. Joanne got very nervous—and I did, too. I feared that something had happened to one of our other boys, Michael, Christopher, or Richard. I stepped off the bus and told Joanne to stay there, but she followed me, hanging on my arm.

I was taken to a phone booth and put in touch with a hospital in Providence. I asked what was wrong and they said they wanted to tell us in person. I told them I was still about 45 minutes away from Providence and demanded to know what was happening. I spoke with Dr. Joe Flynn, who was crying. He told me, through his tears, that Daniel had died. He said it was crib death, or Sudden Infant Death Syndrome, also known as SIDS. I couldn't repeat the words, not with Joanne right next to me. Finally, I hung up the phone and whispered to her that Daniel had died. She literally passed out in my arms by the side of the road, overcome with grief.

We were rushed to the hospital and led into the emergency room. What I saw there was one of the most painful sights of my life: a little, lifeless baby on a long ER bed. Our baby. Joanne fell apart, crying and hugging him. She was blaming herself for leaving him, when it really wasn't her fault at all. SIDS could have happened at any time. While she was embracing Daniel and talking to him through her tears, I honestly didn't know what to say or do. I just wished, at that moment, that I wasn't on this earth; it was the lowest moment of my life.

We had just gone from a euphoric feeling with the team to this unthinkably sad moment by ourselves. I wanted to comfort Joanne, but I didn't have the words or the deeds to do so. I was helpless in terms of knowing how to handle that tragedy.

When we had the funeral, I was touched to look around and see many of my friends in the coaching profession—guys like Jim Boeheim of Syracuse and P. J. Carlesimo, then with Seton Hall. Even at this very busy time of year for basketball coaches, they were there to support us. Still, my heart was ripped open again at the sight of Daniel's tiny infant casket. It symbolized everything to me: how helpless he'd been, and how he never got to grow and experience life. To this day, I still have vivid flashbacks of that casket and the sight of him in the hospital.

In the midst of our mourning, Joanne convinced me to coach the team in the NCAA tournament. I'm glad she did. We had worked so hard for so long to get there—but more than that, it gave me something to hold on to and something to occupy my mind. This was my first encounter with a severe tragedy, and I did not know how to cope with it. I was completely numb, and I think I stayed that way for six months.

When it's the death of a baby, you keep asking why. As a coach, you like to think you have all the right answers, but I had absolutely no answers to that question. I was very confused. I doubted my own Catholic faith and the reason for my existence— but I've learned over time that while my faith was being tested, it also was being strengthened. Today I no longer ask why Daniel died. I just wonder what it would have been like to have him alive.

After Daniel died, I submerged my grief by watching films of our NCAA opponents—first UAB, then Austin Peay. In our hotel room, Joanne and I did not talk much. Neither of us knew what to say or do to make each other feel better. The team rallied around us and helped pick us up. They were constantly checking on our family, asking if we were OK. A close group became even closer, bonding around this tragedy. We kept winning, improbably reaching the Final Four as a No. 6 seed, upsetting Georgetown to get there. It was such an incredible collision of conflicting emotions.

After that season, I was offered a dream job for a New Yorker: to coach the Knicks. I accepted, reluctantly leaving a school I'd grown to love. We also had to leave behind Daniel, who was buried in Providence.

Just before we moved to New York, we took the whole family to the cemetery. That morning at breakfast, our two oldest boys, Michael and Christopher, had been continuing a long-running argument over who had the better baseball card: Michael had a Don Mattingly card; Chris had one of Rickey Henderson. They were crazy about baseball cards at that age. I got angry with them for arguing over something like that on a day when we were going to say good-bye to their departed brother.

When we reached the grave site, I dug a hole and left a St. Christopher medal in the ground. (In our Catholic religion, St. Christopher is the patron saint of sports and travel.) When I turned to go, I saw that my sons had dug their own hole and were burying their Don Mattingly and Rickey Henderson baseball cards. I looked at my children, leaving their most prized possessions in the ground, and was deeply moved. I understood that I needed to cherish them. That taught me, for the first time, how to handle this tragedy.

I would need those lessons again later in life.

Fourteen years later, very shortly after I took the job at Louisville, Joanne and I received jarring news that our brother-in-law, Don Vogt, had been killed in a random street accident in New York City. Don had been at a retirement party for a coworker and had a voucher for a free ride home. He gave it to a coworker, and went out to hail a cab for himself. While standing on the street, a recklessly driven taxi struck and killed this devoted husband and father.

Once again, there was no good explanation. No reason why. To this day, every time I take a taxi in New York or see one weaving in and out of traffic, the only thing I can think of is Don Vogt. It's not a bitterness; it's a realization that life can be snatched away in an instant for reasons we'll never understand. Those are hard realizations to come by.

We learned that again several months after Don died, on 9/11. If possible, Billy Minardi's death hurt Joanne and me even more than the death of Daniel. We had only five months with Daniel, and we'd had decades of wonderful moments with Billy, dating back to our adolescence. From the time I met Joanne during high school on Long Island, her brother Billy had been along for the ride. We went to the races at Saratoga together, went on golfing vacations together. All of my coaching friends knew Billy, because he was always around. Even living in New York, he was a regular at our games when I coached at Kentucky, both home and away. Our relationship was literally every bit as close as my relationship with Joanne. Some people find that hard to believe, but it's true. We both dearly loved Billy, his wife, Stephanie, and their three children—and that's why this tragedy was so hard on us. From the day of his death forward, my life changed forever.

I go around the country speaking on the power of positive thinking, but I also admit that my life will never be as good as when Billy was alive. There are many great moments, especially concerning family matters, but my life will never be complete again. That's the sense of deep, abiding loss so many families victimized by 9/11 went through.

However, even this most personal and painful negative can be turned into a positive. Some of the joy will never be there, but it has been replaced by greater perspective; a greater caring for others and greater appreciation for the world beyond basketball. You have to pick yourself up—and help others pick themselves up, too.

At the time of 9/11, I was getting close to 50 years old and had just come through the fallout from resigning with the Celtics. Age and lessons learned from those events have made me wiser. Specifically, I could see that there is more to this world than basketball. Basketball is my passion; it's been my life since age 7. It's still my passion, but it's no longer my life. After 9/11, I changed the way I think, the way I meet people, the way I can help. Giving to others trumps any form of taking. I'm working, on a daily basis, to put others before me. I've tried to turn my energies outward as much as possible.

That doesn't mean I don't relish being a head coach and a leader, and having a positive effect on my players' lives. It's just that I simply don't need as much praise and recognition anymore. The joy I now get revolves around seeing my family and players succeed and build happiness. Three small things now take on extra meaning in my life:

1.  **Laughter.** I'm in search of any way I can find laughter in my life. I spent so much of my time with Billy just laughing and enjoying everything we did—now I'm looking for ways to fill that void.

    One of the best ways to find a daily laugh is calling my old friend Ralph Willard, a former assistant of mine and now the head coach at Holy Cross. Even with our busy schedules, Ralph and I make time to talk every day, and not all about basketball. We'll argue about the final episode of *The Sopranos*, about the Yankees, about politics and world events. I cherish those 10 or 15 minutes every day talking to Ralph. All these little moments I cherish. I don't take them for granted anymore.

2.  **Humility.** 9/11 made me totally cognizant of other people and not myself. Before that date, I would wonder, "Should I be a pro coach? Should I try to make more money?" None of that even comes into my thinking anymore. Instead it's, "How can I help my children? My nephews and nieces who lost their

fathers?" My whole day is not consumed with how I can succeed, but with how I can help others succeed.

That's why Joanne and I urged Billy's widow and children to move from their home in Bedford, New York, to Louisville several years ago—so they can be near family, and so we could help them get on with their lives. We convinced Stephanie everyone would be happier here. Only my oldest nephew fought it a little bit, but today he won't even look at a college in the Northeast. He's a Kentuckian like the rest of us, and he's going to school at Indiana University now. Stephanie has an active social life, and her younger two kids go to all the Louisville sporting events.

I talk to my team all the time now about helping others and about being humble. At their young age, with all the adulation they've had, humility is a difficult lifestyle for them to truly embrace. As I've learned, it can be difficult enough later in life, but there's nothing I'm doing right now that's very significant, except when I step out and understand how I can help other people grow.

3. **Emotional catharsis.** When you release your emotions, a new energy comes from that release. When you bottle them up, you inhibit your energy and keep everything inside of you. When adversity hits us, we're always affected emotionally. Adversity can bring out the best in us or the worst, depending on the choices we make. So many times in life, we make the wrong choice about how to handle our emotions and, consequently, our actions. Most of us do not want to confront

the pain that comes with adversity. Our inclination is to run away from the pain—to enter denial, to medicate with drugs or alcohol, to escape from the reality of the situation.

When you confront your adversity and that pain head on, your recovery time is much shorter. You're not delaying the inevitable. You're accelerating the process of getting back to normal, and back to a positive frame of mind.

More than six years after 9/11, someone sent me a picture of Billy, myself, and our friend Ron Carmicle at Churchill Downs. We were studying the racing program, and you could tell from the look on our faces that we weren't winning any money. I told Joanne about the picture and she said, "Is this going to make me cry?" To this day, Joanne and I will still get teary-eyed when we talk about Billy—and that's OK. In fact, it's better than my emotionally restrained way of dealing with Daniel's death. Painful as it was, we learned something from that experience.

We acknowledge today that the ache from Billy's death is still there, that it's going to be there, and we're not denying it to ourselves. We're still undergoing a catharsis, still helping each other through it.

In addition to those three things, we've taken a few steps to make sure Billy's name is never forgotten. The dorm where our players live is called Billy Minardi Hall, and every year we have a tournament called the Billy Minardi Classic. We try to have as many friends and family members as possible in town for that event, to celebrate Billy's life and how much he meant to us.

We tried to do something similar in Daniel's honor. We started the Daniel Pitino Foundation to benefit poor and needy children and have raised more than $4 million in Daniel's name. We also opened the Daniel Pitino Shelter in Owensboro for the homeless.

We are trying to turn terrible negatives into positives, while honoring those we dearly miss. That helps, but it doesn't erase everything that has happened—especially the senseless murder of Billy in the terrorist attack.

I try to be as intelligent a person as possible, but the bitterness never leaves—bitterness that Osama bin Laden has never been caught. It preys on us all the time. There's a sickness out there that must be dealt with—an epidemic. As an American, it's difficult to understand the hatred. No matter how much I try to forgive, certain things cannot be forgiven and the bitterness does not go away. I can understand how others might feel about losing a loved one in a drunk-driving accident, or to a tainted medical product, or in some other random circumstance. You want to lash out. You want someone to pay—but revenge is an unproductive emotion and motivation. Revenge is not bringing Billy back, so we chose a different path and have tried to ease the pain of those suffering.

It's still hard. Between our homes in New York, Florida, and Kentucky, there are more than 150 pictures of Billy. Every picture we have, Billy was in them. Every morning when we wake up, we see a huge portrait that a friend, Lynne Carmicle, painted of Billy and myself. Every morning when I have a cup of coffee or a bite to eat, there's Billy staring down at me. In our bedroom, there are 10 pictures of Billy. Downstairs there are 10 more pictures. With all these visual reminders of the past, I must convince myself to think of all the great times. We do that, but there are also moments—at least 50 times a year—where I'll turn to Joanne and say, 'How much do you miss Willie?' We'll talk about it a little bit, just to get it out there. You've got to take it head on, understand what happened, and then celebrate the man.

I learned that lesson from my wife's family. She's half Italian and half Irish. You go to an Italian wake, everyone's bawling and being hysterical. All the women want to jump in the coffin. The Irish, they go to a bar, drink, and talk about the good times and celebrate that person. I'm a *paisan* through and through, but after going to some of those funerals, I subscribe to the Irish wake more than the Italian version.

That's why I loved what my wife did on the day of our biggest win at Louisville. We were playing West Virginia in Albuquerque in the 2005 regional finals, with the winner going to the Final Four. Louisville had not been to the Final Four since 1986, and this win would be a huge milestone in our rebuilding of the program.

We were picked to win, but the Mountaineers came out absolutely on fire. They made everything they threw up—banking in three-pointers, making deep threes, hitting shots with hands in their faces. Joanne was back home in Louisville, watching the game on TV with our future daughter-in-law, Bethany, who was engaged to our oldest son, Michael. As we fell behind by a staggering 20 points in the first half, Joanne brought Billy in from the bullpen. She went into the next room and pulled down that portrait of Billy, painted from a photograph taken on that Pebble Beach trip. She set the portrait in a chair facing the TV and said, "You're going to help us through this."

That was her Irish side coming out.

We began a long comeback, eventually winning the game in overtime and advancing to the Final Four. Joanne talked to Billy throughout that nail-biting game. When we won and cut down the nets, we were euphoric, as were all the Louisville fans who made the long trip to New Mexico. And back home, so was Joanne.

Our charter flight returned in the wee hours of the morning and when I arrived home, the portrait was still sitting in the chair, staring at the TV. The next morning, the story of the portrait was shared. Joanne told me how Billy watched the game with her and Bethany, coaxing them (and us) through our comeback. We shared a few tears, and then we laughed. Billy, I'm sure, would have approved.

## Gaining Perspective

**REBOUND RULES:**

- **Tragedy will test you like nothing else.** Keep your faith and rely on it to help you through—even if you're questioning it at the time.

- **Let your emotions out, and work through them.** Catharsis is necessary to avoid bitterness.

- **Turn your grief into good.** Let your hard-earned new perspective be the catalyst to a more humble, charitable you.

**POINTS OF CAUTION:**

- **Don't demand answers to the inexplicable.** Sometimes there are none.

- **Don't miss the lessons you can learn in these trying moments.** A child's act of grace—leaving a cherished object at a gravesite—can teach you so much.

- **Don't marinate in bitterness or preoccupy yourself with revenge.** Both are unproductive.

Chapter Three

# PHD

**J**AMAL MASHBURN WAS THE FIRST player I recruited to the University of Kentucky, and ultimately probably the best. When he turned pro after his junior season in 1993, I wanted to help "Mash" invest his money wisely, so I started searching for a Wall Street firm that would set him up for long-term growth. I asked several friends who work on Wall Street to give me their personal top-five lists of investors. One name kept appearing on the lists: Mario Gabelli, now the CEO of GAMCO Investors, Inc. I wound up visiting him to discuss what he could do for Jamal.

He gave me a tour of his office in Rye, New York, and at the core of his business center were about 200 people working on trading equities and bonds. The focus and determination was evident.

"Mario," I asked, "what kind of people do you look to hire? Wharton grads? University of Chicago? Harvard business school?"

"I couldn't care less where they went to school," he said. "I look for PHDs."

"That's a little unusual for your line of work," I responded.

"I recruit Poor, Hungry, and Driven people," he said.

Since then I've used that term over and over with my teams, because it captured the essence of what I wanted them to be: never smug, never satisfied, always wanting to improve and reach their full potential. However, I decided—with the help of one of my current players—to modify my PHD slogan. Terrence Williams didn't grow up with much in the way of material comforts in Seattle. One day, after hearing another in a series of PHD pep talks, he finally asked me, "Look, can we lose the 'Poor'?"

I understood. Aspiring professional basketball players don't want to hear about being poor, even as a metaphor for something else. So "Poor" is out and "Passionate" is in, and I like the updated slogan even more than the original. Because if there is one thing that makes coaching basketball as fun for me now in my mid-50s as it was in my mid-20s, it's passion. Passion for the game, passion for the competition, passion for helping young men grow up, passion for creating team success through the collaboration of individuals. That has never gone away—if anything it has gotten stronger.

The PHD mentality is a common denominator of all successful people. When you're faced with adversity, you have to go back to that attitude. When you're enjoying success, you have to maintain it without embracing it. Every single day as a businessperson—good days or bad—you have to project a passionate, hungry, and driven outlook. Sell yourself on it, and infect those around you with it. Without it, you cannot be successful.

After the Celtics job unraveled, in order to rebound successfully I had to get back to my personal fundamentals—my own

PHD. In dealing with the deaths our family has endured, my PHD helped provide a meaningful distraction in times of grief and bitterness. It has been a valuable resource throughout my adult life—and never more valuable than when trying to rebound from a significant setback.

Let's break down the PHD by each of its three ingredients:

## PASSION

There are a number of professionals who struggle to stir their passion. They can't necessarily be who they want to be—an athlete, an actor, someone living a glamorous life outside the grind of 9 to 5. They'll listen to me talk and say, "Well, it's easy for you. You're a basketball coach. You have a great job, great perks." Well, it's not about that. Whatever job you have, it's up to you to be passionate about it and make that job a great one. It doesn't matter whether you're a crossing guard, a schoolteacher, or a basketball coach. It might not be where you want to be tomorrow, but it's where you are today. Seize the day.

How can you have passion if you're doing a job that you're not in love with? That's where you've got to change. You have to alter your belief in your job. If you can't change jobs, you have to change your opinion of your job. Tom Sawyer didn't want to whitewash a fence, but he made it appear so important and rewarding that others—starting with his friend Ben—paid him for the chance to do it themselves:

> "Say—I'm going in a-swimming, I am," Ben said. "Don't you wish you could? But of course you'd druther *work*— wouldn't you? Course you would!"
>
> Tom contemplated the boy a bit, and said:

"What do you call work?"

"Why, ain't *that* work?"

Tom resumed his whitewashing, and answered carelessly:

"Well, maybe it is, and maybe it ain't. All I know, is, it suits Tom Sawyer."

"Oh come, now, you don't mean to let on that you *like* it?"

The brush continued to move.

"Like it? Well, I don't see why I oughtn't to like it. Does a boy get a chance to whitewash a fence every day?"

In truth, Tom Sawyer was delegating work to his unwitting peers by selling it as fun—but sometimes you have to sell yourself on your own work. If whitewashing a fence—or something similarly uninspiring—is your job, embrace it as the one task you have the opportunity to perform perfectly today. Aspire to be the best whitewasher in the business, to make that fence your Sistine Chapel.

When we coach individual instruction workouts with our players in the mornings, I try to be as involved, as thorough and as demanding of the 10th guy on our team as I am of the star. My job during those 42 minutes is to teach basketball fundamentals and reinforce the tenets of our specific system. My job is to help that player improve. If I'm a professional, I give those 42 minutes my maximum effort and concentration—because that's my job, and that's my task of the moment. We have one chance to do our best on each given day; don't waste that chance. Personally, I would hate to reach old age and look back with regret on a life full of days spent half-stepping, or just trying to get by instead of trying to be great.

When I was a young assistant coach, I never allowed myself the time to complain about a low salary, long hours, or the unglamorous life of recruiting. Back then you could recruit virtually year-round, so we were all over the map, watching players and trying to convince them to come to our school. It was exhausting at times. Those nights of bad hotels, drive-thru food, and endless phone calls were not easy—but I loved every minute of it. I took the title literally: I was an assistant, there to assist the team by any means requested or required. I understood my role: to assist the head coach, assist the players—something I tell all my assistants to this day. They're vital and valuable, and I appreciate the work they do, but they must accept the reality of what their position calls for.

For me, I understood that I was to be seen and not heard, and to work like a dog. This was not the period in my life to seek recognition; it was a time to learn the profession I'd chosen. It's vital for young professionals to accept a supporting role, embrace it, and learn everything they can from it before moving on to bigger and better. It's also vital for their superiors to cultivate their talents and keep them in their place at the same time. Encourage their progress, but don't reward them for average work.

One of my top five memories in 30 years as a coach were the two I spent as an assistant to Hubie Brown with the Knicks in the 1980s. I was challenged each day by a brilliant boss who wanted to help me grow but made me earn my stripes. Hubie taught me the value of being ultra-prepared, of embracing the details, of coaching the fundamentals. I soaked up everything I saw. I threw myself into the job, determined to be the best assistant coach I could be. That's the way I woke up every day—eager, determined, passionate—and that had to do with my own self-esteem. I felt good about myself and what I was doing for a living. I cannot stress enough how important a positive message is to achieving success.

Here's an illustration: I recently gave my players a talk about the importance of making great grades. I told them they need an education to fall back on if they get hurt or something goes wrong in their basketball career. I told them their college careers should be built on a tripod—one leg is education, one leg is basketball, and the third is discipline; you need discipline to do well in the other two areas.

However, I didn't deliver the message correctly. Here's what I said to my team: "You guys aren't all going to be professional basketball players. You have to start paying attention to your academics, getting better grades, because you're not going to make it in the basketball world. You have to understand what the real world is all about." Well, one player came to me at the end of the season and said he was thinking about transferring. He took that conversation to mean that I didn't think he could be a pro. That's what they listened to—the negative message.

I told him, "You don't understand the message I was trying to give. You can certainly be a pro, and you certainly should work toward that goal. But you're not achieving success in the classroom, and that's what you have to fall back on." It wasn't until that follow-up conversation that he understood: I wasn't trying to kill his dreams; I was trying to broaden his scope. When I explained it to him, he dropped his plans to transfer and decided to stay at Louisville.

The better initial message would have been this: "A lot of you guys are going to make it in the basketball world, and that's great.

I want to encourage you to fight for it. Strive for it. Do whatever you can to get there. But along the way you must not shortchange your education." The message is exactly the same, but it's a different way of expressing it. One was building self-esteem, the other was lowering it. Communicating in a way that sends a positive message is vital.

That's why I've come to believe that it's imperative to follow team meetings with individual meetings—to make sure each person gets the message you want them to get. Because it's amazing how many different interpretations you can have from one meeting.

From that academic meeting, one player was convinced I doubted his basketball ability. Another player, full of false confidence, knew I couldn't have been speaking to him about needing a Plan B if basketball didn't work out. A third player wasn't sure the meeting pertained to him at all.

Bottom line: Don't let the message get lost in translation. Be your own messenger, instead of entrusting your message to someone who doesn't know it as well as you do. Follow up individually and hammer your point home—because it's surprisingly easy to create doubt if you send the wrong message. If you want your workforce to have passion for jobs they don't love, you have to build their self-esteem, provide them feedback, and model enthusiasm in the workplace.

In other words, show passion. Find inspiration in the lifelong passion of Billy Graham for the next crusade, of Robert DeNiro for the next acting role, of Joe Paterno for the next football game. Those are the men I admire—the greats who could quit at any time with their legacy secure, but they love what they do too much to walk away. Their passion is fed by an endless hunger.

## HUNGER

What happens when you eat that big meal on Thanksgiving Day? You get sluggish. You want to take a nap. You want to shut down. That's what can happen when you experience success in business and sports as well. Most people who achieve success have pushed very hard to get there, often for decades. When you break through and make the big sale or earn the big promotion, the natural human reaction is to feast on the glory, get sluggish, and shut down.

You start enjoying the fruits of your labor. In this microwave culture, boom, you're done. Hey, everyone takes vacations. Everyone gets downtime. Those are necessary and important. It's when downtime and vacation encroach into your normal work habits that it becomes a danger—and it happens all the time. Coaches stop working as hard in recruiting. Players don't put in the extra time in the gym. Businesspeople turn the weekly round of golf into three rounds a week—cutting into their sales calls to do it.

Remember Buster Douglas, the boxer? He pulled off one of the biggest upsets in sports history when he knocked out the previously invincible Mike Tyson in 1990 in Tokyo. That was Buster's breakthrough moment—and also the moment he quit working at his craft. He literally got fat and happy. After becoming heavyweight champion, Douglas had just one title defense, a listless third-round knockout at the fists of Evander Holyfield. He retired on the fat payday from that fight, plumped up to nearly 400 pounds, and didn't do much for several years. He made a half-hearted comeback attempt in the late 1990s, and hasn't been heard from this century.

Hopefully he invested well.

There are one-hit wonders in all walks of life. Popular music is filled with bands who delivered a single song that roared up the charts, then they were never heard from again. Hunger, or a lack of it after cashing in commercially, could be part of the disappearing act. I don't know whether a lack of hunger kept authors Harper Lee (*To Kill a Mockingbird*), Margaret Mitchell (*Gone with the Wind*), or Ralph Ellison (*The Invisible Man*) from ever writing a second novel, but their talents were missed after that one great effort.

Comedian Dave Chappelle was a spectacular hit for a few years in his early 30s, but pressure or burnout or a lack of hunger sent him walking away from his lucrative HBO show in 2006. He's never returned to regular television appearances. Similarly, the world has waited for years for another great comedian, Jerry Seinfeld, to resume making us laugh on a regular basis. Considering that Seinfeld reportedly made $267 million off his TV show in 1998 alone, there isn't a lot of monetary incentive to resume hustling.

Then there are those at the opposite extreme. Tiger Woods is as relentless today as he was in 1997, when he won his first Masters. He's the richest athlete in the world, but he prepares like the hungriest—and that's a huge reason why he keeps winning. Nothing more perfectly illustrated Tiger's continuing hunger to be the best than what he did in winning the 2008 U.S. Open at Torrey Pines, playing 91 holes with a double stress fracture and a torn anterior cruciate ligament in his left knee. He could have withdrawn from that tournament at any time and nobody would have blamed him, but he didn't. That's why Tiger is revered and respected worldwide. Peyton Manning is another example. He finally won the Super Bowl in 2007, but the next day he knew the exact date of the Colts' first off-season weight workout and vowed to be there. I loved hearing that.

I admire people like journalist David Halberstam, who kept his hunger over a tremendously long period of time. Halberstam published his first book in 1961 and his last in 2007, with 20 others in between, covering subjects from war to politics to sports. He also worked as an influential newspaper writer for the *New York Times*. At the time of his death in an automobile accident in 2007 at age 73, he was working on another book. Actor Henry Fonda's career was similar. He began his acting career in his home state of Nebraska at age 20, made his first film at age 30, and won an Academy Award for Best Actor for his work in *On Golden Pond* at age 76, not long before his death.

A good word that goes with staying hungry is staying humble. Lack of humility is the greatest killer of potential with young people. It's unfortunate that most of us don't find humility until around 50 years of age. By then, most of us have hit enough potholes to know that we don't always have all the answers. The Celtics situation helped reinforce that to me—my first inclination was to beat myself up for failing, but ultimately I turned that lost self-esteem into newfound modesty. After receiving a great deal of personal blame for not turning around the franchise, it became clear that I'd probably received too much personal credit for the previous successes in my career. As my good friend and thoroughbred trainer Nick Zito likes to say, "Before honor, humility."

Too often, early success leads us to believe that we've arrived. Suddenly we stop trying to improve ourselves, and we stagnate. You see it all the time. Rap stars, rock stars, successful Wall Street people, successful sports people—if they're young, they're generally not very humble. They may talk about being humble, but many of them are only paying lip service to it. With basketball players, you can see it in how they carry themselves on and off the court. How do they interact with coaches, teammates, referees, and fans? You can tell by their interactions whether they feel superior to those around them.

In talking to firms and trying to get them to hire my players, they always point out their desire to hire team players. More important than GPA or major, they want someone willing to put the company's goals before their own. They'll accept lower abilities in order to get the motivated person who fits into the larger concept. In the *Wall Street Journal*/Harris Interactive 2007 rankings of the top MBA programs, Dartmouth's Tuck School of Business finished first in a survey of recruiters, while Harvard was 14th and Stanford was 19th. I was surprised to see that—until I read the recruiters' comments on the schools. "Tuck students live and breathe teamwork," one recruiter told the *Journal*. "The admissions process requires applicants to have a demonstrated excellence in teamwork, and then the faculty, curriculum, and culture inculcate a practical understanding of teamwork at every step of the Tuck experience."

Meanwhile, the *Journal* story said Harvard and Stanford "again were criticized for what recruiters said were their students' inflated egos and excessive expectations." In short, they weren't developing humble, hungry, team-oriented young people.

In 30 years as a coach, I've developed a fairly keen eye for when players have let success get to their heads. You can see it if they stop coming into the gym for extra shooting practice, or if they're no longer going all-out in every sprint during conditioning drills, or if they get frustrated when their scoring dips for a game or two. When that happens, we'll bring them back down to earth.

That's why our practices after we win can sometimes be harder than after we lose. During film sessions, we'll praise them for what they did well—but we'll also drill home the mistakes, then test their focus on the court. If they don't come out ready to work hard after a good game, we tighten the screws. That's trying to maintain hunger and humility.

The sooner young people find humility, the easier it becomes for them to be successful. Still, it cannot be forced, and experience is the best teacher. You see it in later years, in the older coaches. The person who epitomized it most was John Wooden— but he found it at a very young age, as did Dean Smith, the Hall of Fame North Carolina coach.

Young coaches would be wise to look at successful people like Wooden and Smith who stood the test of time. They would be wise to accept feedback without bristling, to understand how other people made their mark and then sustained a level of excellence. Everyone thinks they have a degree of humility, but they don't—and then when they start talking to other people, they find out the truth. Seeking out feedback can be a great way to grow.

When I was a young coach, I would read some articles that were pretty complimentary, but the word "arrogant" would come up. My initial response would be to say, "That's BS. I'm not arrogant. Just ask my friends and family members." But asking my friends and family members wouldn't always elicit an objective response. They love me, and they're not going to always give me honest feedback—and you want honest feedback. I finally conceded: If that's the way I was being perceived, there might be truth to it. It may not be 100 percent, may not be 80 percent, but there's some truth to it. I needed to accept that criticism and learn from it.

Another method of accepting humility can come when we fail. If you're not accustomed to it, your first instinct might be to blame it on something or someone else. Surely it couldn't be your fault, could it? If you can objectively examine what happened, you might come to find that you're not perfect, and have room for improvement. The key is objective self-analysis, and being open to honest outside feedback.

To be truly open to the critiques of others, you must have developed the ability to listen. Listening is learning. Hear every voice that contains some value to you. Don't interrupt them, and don't spend your time thinking of what you're going to say next—actually listen to the points they're making. Soak it in. It takes practice to fully lock in on someone and what they're saying: practice and patience.

We have to train ourselves to make listening a singular task, not something that's done while we're busy with something else. These days, we as Americans are so busy multitasking that our listening seems to be at an all-time low. We're reading e-mails while talking on the phone. We're texting someone while in the company of others. Here's irony for you: Amid the avalanche of new communication methods, truly productive two-way conversation is becoming a lost art. If you can't take the time to listen to feedback, you're not going to get better.

A lot of coaches say, "Accept coaching, accept criticism, because that's a way of getting better"—but then *they* can't accept it. You can't be that way. If you're going to have humility, you must accept the criticism and accept the heat—because you're dishing it out all the time as leaders. Humility is part of being hungry.

## DRIVE

You organize your drive each and every day. It doesn't just happen. You don't just say, "I'm driven, let's go." You don't get in the car, turn it on, and drive to nowhere. You're driving to a place, a destination. Being driven is all about being organized.

The first thing you do is decide where you want to get to—both long term and short term. You set goals for yourself: career goals in the big picture; daily goals in the smaller picture. Then you keep track of how you do reaching those goals.

My daily routine facilitates my drive. It is organized and as close to airtight as I can make it—there isn't much dead time built in, because dead time rarely helps you attain those daily goals. I demand a lot of my staff, and it can be a culture shock sometimes for the new guys—but once they get into the routine and establish good working habits, it pays off. An organized plan of attack helps everyone.

To keep my schedule as organized as possible, I write it all down on a daily basis. This is an idea I borrowed from my old boss Hubie Brown, who wrote down everything—he'd take notes on phone conversations, and would refer back to them weeks later. Hubie wrote his daily duties on a notebook page divided in half: calls he had to make, other duties to perform, and things to improve. What didn't get done on Monday, he moved across the page to his list for Tuesday. I've modified that system, using my trusty note cards and a blue pen I carry with me at all times. At the end of the day, I review what happened, and I circle in red everything that didn't get done and needs to carry over to tomorrow. Then I chart the next day before I go to bed.

I've learned better than to leave it up to memory. Passing thoughts and sudden ideas need to be written down, or else I'll forget. If I'm recruiting a player and I go watch his high school team practice, when I leave the gym, I'll grab a card and jot down what I saw or something that came up in conversation with his coach. Then I can refer back to those things when I write a follow-up note or make a follow-up phone call. Details, details, details.

If I'm not in a place where I can write something down—say, in the car—I'll keep a tape recorder handy. There have been several occasions when I've used the tape recorder to gather my thoughts for a motivational talk to my team or points of emphasis in a pregame press conference.

Most days during the season, I'll get up at about 5:45. I'm an early riser. Optimists can't wait to get going. Self-initiative is absolutely vital if you're going to reach for lofty goals and work your way through adversity whenever it arises. After waking up, I immediately go straight to the elliptical or treadmill and do 15 or 20 minutes quickly to get my juices flowing. That's not my workout—it's just a quick calorie burn, a chance to think my way through the day ahead, then I jump in the shower. I'll have some fruit, then on the way to the office, I usually drive by Starbucks, get my cappuccino, and get into work between 6:30 or 6:40. I advocate living close to the office if possible; too many people lose time and add frustration being caught in traffic during long commutes.

When I arrive at the office, I always want to attack the most difficult problems first. It's the only way for me to approach it. If you let something slip until the afternoon, you're likely to let it slip until the next day—and the next day—and the next. Pretty soon it's hanging over you like an anvil, because you didn't attack it head-on when the problem first presented itself. In fact, scientific studies have shown that this is the most effective way to work through a day. Your brain consumes a huge amount of energy, and attempting to tackle difficult tasks late in the day is difficult because your brain is low on energy. All the more reason to take care of the hardest stuff early and the less-complicated work later.

So my daily agenda begins with the toughest and most tedious tasks, then proceeds to our morning business meeting in the 7 o'clock hour. A couple things I've learned about productive meetings: They are not a gathering place for idle conversation; they're not a minute longer than they need to be; and they must be followed by action. Everyone on my staff should walk out of the meeting ready to act, not asking what just transpired. If they don't come away with a clear vision of what to do next, it wasn't a productive meeting.

Our morning staff meetings are rarely longer than 30 minutes, then it's on to individual player instruction. This is another area where my passion for my job still shows through. I love working with players individually on improving the fundamentals of their game. Each player goes hard for 42 minutes through a rigorous set of drills—I'm there watching and coaching everything, and we have a manager assigned to chart all the data on shots taken and missed. My intensity during these drills is evident, and it usually transfers to the players. They know better than to come in unfocused for individual workouts. Our players tend to improve their skill level significantly during their college careers, and this is where it happens most—in these individual instruction sessions.

My staff and I run those workouts for 42 minutes every hour, from 8 through 11 A.M. Then at noon, I'm continuing my own workout regimen—I used to run on the treadmill every day, but a knee injury has moved me to lower-impact work. After a shower, I might grab a cup of soup, but I'm usually not much of a lunch eater.

Now that I'm 56, I am making some allowances for fatigue in my daily schedule—knowing your limits and working around them is an important part of avoiding burnout or physical problems. For example, I've scaled back my midday workout regimen to account for aching knees—more walking and less running. That's another way I'm learning to be humble: I've come to accept the fact that my body is no longer indestructible. Sleep is more important now. If I don't take care of myself, I'll break down more easily. I'm not 25 anymore, and there's no need to pretend I am. You can make concessions to age without capitulating entirely.

We generally have an afternoon team meeting, watch some film, then we practice from 3 to 5:15 P.M. After that, we'll get together one more time as a staff to talk about practice, review any tape or statistics from that, and prepare for the next day.

It's at this time that I do something a little bit different than I have in the past: I send my assistants home. Many years ago, when I had an all-star staff at Kentucky, two of my assistants came to me saying they were working too hard. They were Herb Sendek, who has gone on to be a very successful head coach at Miami (Ohio), North Carolina State, and Arizona State, and Billy Donovan, who went on to win consecutive national championships at Florida. It was March, and they were in the office until 9 or 10 at night, every night. Considering the fact that they were getting to the office before dawn, their wives were not happy with this. To this day, I believe Billy put Herb up to it. Herb was higher up the ladder at that point so he did the talking.

"Coach, we're burning out a little bit. Billy and I were wondering whether we could get a little more time off, spend more time with our families," Herb said.

"Why aren't you spending time with your families?" I asked.

"Because we're here all night watching film," Herb replied.

So we reached a solution. I didn't demand anything less from them—I just told them to go home around dinner time, spend some time with the family, and then work from home later at night. Watch your film at home, make your recruiting calls, but get your family time in first.

You can't be successful, in business and in sports, having a dys-functional family. Too many problems arise and seep into your day. If your spouse is unhappy, you're going to be unhappy, too, and less productive. Your family has to be part of the success story.

So now, at 6 o'clock, everyone goes home. That's family time. Go home and have dinner with them; spend some quality time with the kids. When they go to bed, it's time to go back to work and do your thing. With my family, we go out to eat a lot, then often times we'll go home and watch a game together on TV. Sometimes, for the sake of domestic tranquility, I will watch *Law & Order* with Joanne. Concessions must be made, you know.

When they go to bed, I'll watch *SportsCenter* or I'll surf for a West Coast game or an NBA game with a team I enjoy watching—always with a note card and pen sitting next to me, in case I see something I think can be incorporated into our game plan. If need be, I might break down a little film of an upcoming opponent.

And when the alarm clock goes off at 5:45 the next morning, I'm ready to go through the routine again. Why? Because I have passion for my job, hunger to succeed, and a drive to do whatever it will take to achieve that success. The next rule is adding a dose of patience to that PHD when everyone around you is screaming for immediate results.

## *PHD*

### REBOUND RULES:

+ **Be passionate.** Strive to be the best at what you do, no matter what you're doing. Whitewash that fence with pride and enthusiasm.

+ **Be hungry.** Don't let the first taste of success spoil your appetite for more. Sustain your hunger over the course of your career.

+ **Be driven.** Meticulously organize and aim your drive toward your goals.

### POINTS OF CAUTION:

+ **Don't work as if you're overqualified for your job.** If you believe that day's task is beneath you, you'll perform it in subpar fashion.

+ **Don't bring arrogance to a group venture.** Be a team player and accept your role.

+ **Don't go a million miles an hour without a plan.** It's one thing to work hard; it's a better thing to work hard with an eye on specific results and accomplishments.

# Chapter Four

# Surviving and Thriving in the Microwave Culture

**I**'M AN IMPATIENT PERSON. I like basketball and life at a fast
tempo—the more action, the more stimulation, the more
challenges, the better—but I've also learned how to balance
impatience with realism and perspective. I strive for success every
day, but I'm more aware than ever that most of life's important,
long-term goals cannot be achieved at the snap of your fingers or
the click of your mouse—even if society wants it that way.

That's the microwave culture. If you understand it, you can be
successful—and you need to understand it, because it's not changing. If anything, the pace of change will only quicken. Approval
ratings—for presidents with the voting public, CEOs with the
shareholders, and basketball coaches with the fans—are more
fickle than ever, rising and falling daily.

What ushered in the microwave culture? The same thing that
gave us the microwave itself: technology. It has accelerated everything in our lives, from communication to commerce. Technology has changed the way we cook our meals, changed the way

we get information, changed the way we shop. A dinner that once took hours to produce can now be prepared in minutes. Information that used to take days to deliver via traditional mail is now sent in an instant via e-mail or text message. Shopping trips are now conducted with a few clicks of a mouse.

That's changed our habits, and changed our outlook on what it means to wait. We expect information now, gratification now, results now. Nobody waits for tomorrow's paper anymore to check scores or stocks, and nobody remembers what happened yesterday. Why work hard to become noticed when you can simply post a YouTube video and earn a cheap snippet of fame in minutes?

In this era of rapid rewards, there is little thought given to the long haul. Fans don't want to give a coach time to painstakingly develop a program, and shareholders don't want to give a CEO time to painstakingly improve the company's bottom line. We understand, intellectually, that there's no way to be successful by putting something into a microwave and pulling it out, ready-made, in two minutes. That's a fan's perspective. However, as businesspeople you must accept the reality of it. When I started motivational speaking 20 years ago, I was reading all about the Japanese model of business, and it would go out one to five to 10 years forward in planning. That simply does not exist today, in the business world or the sports world. The microwave culture will not allow that type of planning.

When I was with the Boston Celtics from 1997–2000, I succumbed to the microwave culture timetable. I hastily tried to refurbish a depleted team, making trades and roster transactions in rapid succession. I was being paid more than any coach in basketball history, and I felt the only way to earn my salary was by performing an instant turnaround. We didn't have the talent to make that happen, but I put pressure on myself to do it anyway.

What I found out is that you can't trade mediocre players for mediocre players and come up with good players. Trading your problem for someone else's problem doesn't leave you without a problem. It's not going to work. NBA executives don't make rash mistakes and submit to lopsided trades, though you will occasionally see exceptions to that rule. Kevin Garnett *did* walk through that door in Boston in 2007, and Pau Gasol did go to the Los Angeles Lakers to make them a championship contender. (At least Minnesota got a terrific young player from Boston in Al Jefferson; Memphis has to hope the draft picks it got from the Lakers turn out to be superstars.) But in my time with the Celtics, we didn't have much to give in terms of trade value after inheriting a team that went 15–67 the year before, so we made a series of lateral moves that kept us in the same spot.

By seeking instant improvement, everything I did was at warp speed instead of steadily building for the long haul. I overpaid a pair of journeyman free-agent big men, Travis Knight and Andrew DeClercq. In the middle of his rookie year, I traded away a young point guard who has become an NBA All-Star, Chauncey Billups—though I have to point out that three other teams traded Chauncey thereafter. It took him six seasons to develop into the player he is today.

Bottom line: I was so unaccustomed to losing that I tried to short-circuit the rebuilding process and get back to winning. Instead, I wound up delaying our progress. Another lesson learned from failure.

By the time I got to Boston, times had changed from when I

was hired at my previous job, at Kentucky, in 1989. When I went to Kentucky, I inherited a mess: The program was on NCAA probation and under major sanctions that banned us from playing in the Southeastern Conference or NCAA tournaments for two years. We had only eight scholarship players, none of them taller than six feet eight—big by everyday office standards, but scarily small for major-college basketball.

For those reasons, athletic director C. M. Newton gave me an unusually long seven-year contract. He knew how difficult the rebuilding task might be, so he built in extra time to get it done. Fortunately, we didn't need it, advancing to the 1992 NCAA tournament regional finals in our first postseason eligibility and making the Final Four just a year later, but there was an understanding that miracles generally don't happen on demand.

Fast-forward to the 21st century. Alabama's football program faced similarly strict NCAA penalties in the same league, but showed just how much patience has dwindled—not just in sports, but in society as a whole. In 2005, third-year coach Mike Shula led a probation-depleted Crimson Tide team to a surprising 10–2 record and was named SEC Coach of the Year. In 2006, he went 6–6 and was fired.

That is the microwave culture at work.

In 2005, Mississippi fired David Cutcliffe for having the nerve to go 4–7. It was his first losing season in six years at the school, and was just one year removed from a 10–3 season in the toughest football conference in the country. What did that move get the Rebels? It got them Ed Orgeron, the coach hired to replace the understated Cutcliffe. He impressed fans with his bravado and intensity but not with his record: Orgeron was fired after going 7–16 in two seasons.

That is the microwave culture at work.

The ultimate sports example of surviving in the microwave culture might be New York Giants coach Tom Coughlin. In 2006, the Giants struggled to an 8–8 record, including a late six-game losing streak and a first-round playoff loss to Philadelphia. The franchise decision makers thought seriously about firing Coughlin, but in the end they decided to bring him back in 2007 with a one-year contract extension for '08. The reaction was widespread outrage. Virtually every newspaper columnist in New York was calling for Coughlin's head—and the fans agreed. "The noose was around my neck," Coughlin told me, "and they were walking me off the plank."

Even the *New York Times*, which tends to be a very sober sporting publication, was tinged with bloodlust. On the paper's website, fans were asked their opinion on whether Coughlin should be fired. Of the 104 who responded with a definitive yes or no, 86 wanted him gone. Many of them wanted quarterback Eli Manning packing his bags, too. Among the vitriolic reader comments, from a readership generally considered among the most thoughtful in the nation:

> *"Cut the losses and fire the coach. . . . But, the QB has to go also to ever have a Super Bowl contender."—William*

> *"Simply put, TOM COUGHLIN SUCKS. The Giants will never go further than a wild-card loss with him. He is an immature child who loses his temper on field on a weekly basis. He is an embarrassment to the New York Giants organization."—J. Shay*

> *"Let's put it this way: I WILL NO LONGER WATCH GIANTS GAMES TILL Coughlin is FIRED!!!!!!!!!"—Earl*

Poor Earl. If he stayed true to his angry words, he missed Tom Coughlin—and his useless quarterback, Eli—leading the Giants to a thrilling Super Bowl victory over the unbeaten and allegedly unbeatable New England Patriots.

But the Coughlin doubters were around even during the '07 season. When the Giants started off 0–2, fans and media members were ready to give up on the year and the coach. Several media outlets predicted that a third straight loss could result in Coughlin being fired immediately.

As Steve Serby wrote in the *New York Post* after that 0–2 start: "[Coughlin's] team is in trouble again and he is in trouble again.

"He isn't Dead Man Walking yet, but if this keeps up, the plank will be waiting for him.

"The worst possible way for Coughlin to open the 2007 season, given the way his dysfunctional Giants closed the 2006 season, was with The Worst Team in Football."

In the face of that, Coughlin didn't succumb to the microwave culture and melt down. "I still believed in us. I knew we were better than we'd played." His faith was rewarded as the Giants, of course, eventually went from worst to first. They pulled out what bordered on a must-win game against the Washington Redskins in the third week of the year, survived a bumpy home season, squeaked into the playoffs as a wild-card team—and then ran the table, all the way through an epic Super Bowl upset.

In the process, Tom Coughlin outlived and outlasted the microwave culture.

He adjusted his approach a bit from 2006 to 2007, lightening up in dealing with his players and with the media, but Coughlin never deserted his core beliefs about how to coach a football team. He stayed consistent, refusing to panic when the pressure was on. And so the same guy everyone wanted fired a year earlier—and even at the beginning of that same season—wound up holding the Lombardi Trophy come February.

"The principles I believe in did not change," Coughlin said. "The football part of it had to remain the same, and the players never questioned that. I made a list of five things we had to do, and one of those was, 'No Toughness, No Championship.' That was critical. But what I did do was adapt the thought process that the dinosaur could change." Basically, the "dinosaur" devised a two-level plan: He altered his approach with the media and players (a strategy that paid immediate short-term benefits) while maintaining his football convictions for the long term. That's how you deal with the current culture.

Before the season, Coughlin sat down with longtime Giants P.R. head Pat Hanlon to ascertain why the coach engendered so much media antagonism. They decided to have Coughlin meet with all of the New York beat writers behind closed doors, and let everyone air their differences and grievances. Coughlin said the one thing that stuck with him was when a beat writer told him the coach seemed to lack respect for reporters.

"I've always believed in solid American work ethic," Coughlin said, "and the one thing I do not want to be thought of is being disrespectful of a guy who is busting his butt to do his job. That does not mean I agree with the role of the writer, but I decided I'll respect the job they have to do. I'll be more patient. I'm not much on redundancy," he continued. "It's difficult for me not to show my impatience. But I withstood some of the repetitious questions and some questions that weren't very intelligent. I tried to grin and bear it. Even in crisis, I still tried to maintain that."

Coughlin also formed an 11-man team leadership council in an effort to smooth locker-room relations. One player from each position met with Coughlin regularly through the season to, as he put it, "help us, in a more relaxed way, communicate to the players." That paid dividends as well. But the other thing Tom Coughlin did in 2007, at the urging of his family, was to get back in touch with his passion for the game. There was a reason he chose this profession, and during those difficult times he had to reacquaint himself with why he loved football and the fundamentals of what made him a successful coach. "My family told me to enjoy the year. I said, 'You know what? I will. If this is my last year, I'm going to enjoy it.'"

It doesn't get too much more enjoyable than holding up the Vince Lombardi trophy just a year after the microwave culture wanted to run you out of town—but that's life in the NFL. (Which by the way, is rumored to not simply stand for National Football League: It also stands for "Not For Long." Head coaches last an average of just over four years in the league.)

NFL coaches aren't the only professionals trying to survive increasingly rapid turnover, though. According to one study, corporate executives saw their average tenure shrink from about eight years in the early 1990s to 4.7 years by the turn of the century. In coaching, you're only as good as your last game, and on Wall Street, you're only as good as your last trade. There are no long-term contracts, nothing in writing that guarantees your future is secure if you have a bad year or two. It might be the ultimate microwave marketplace.

In that sort of atmosphere, playing for one big score instead of building for consistent success is a chronic temptation. It's a risky business strategy, but in a world of instant demands and instant rewards you see many people try it. People who try for the quick payday and then don't handle setbacks well are not leadership material. You want people with resilience running the show.

Those people were in short supply during the dot-com boom,

which epitomized the effect of the microwave culture on business. An example of the shortsighted nature of that boom is Fogdog, the online sporting goods retailer. It was one of the many buzz companies of the late '90s, with a splashy national advertising campaign, a lucrative deal to sell Nike gear, and an IPO that reeled in $66 million on sales of six million shares in December 1999. "'Fogdog' may soon become a household word," proclaimed the *San Jose Business Journal*. However, that household-name status came with a short shelf life. In less than a year, Fogdog's stock had dipped below $1 per share, and the company reclassified its expenses after being accused of dubious accounting. Global Sports, Inc., finally stepped in and bought its floundering competitor, cutting most of the workforce along the way.

This example of Fogdog was typical of the microwavable terrain of the times. In late 2001, the *Wall Street Journal* compiled a list of 205 Web-related companies that had dramatically cut staff or closed down since 2000.

There were so many of what my friend Mario Gabelli describes as "flavor of the month" companies, trying to make a quick score. San Francisco-based online grocer Webvan built a gigantic infrastructure and planned an expansion to 26 cities— only to close shop after two years and put 2,000 workers out of jobs. DigiScents tried to sell smells over the Internet, with predictable results. Pets.com advertised at the highest level—a Super Bowl spot—but couldn't convince pet owners to buy their goods online. Not even having a Macy's Thanksgiving Day Parade balloon made of its briefly famous sock-puppet dog was enough for Pets.com to stave off insolvency.

Enron might be the ultimate microwave culture company. It was in such a fevered rush for profit that it took every shortcut it could. The result was an epic case of fraud that turned the company into a one-word symbol for the excesses of corporate greed. Investors everywhere were duped.

The latest wave of investors seduced by quick and easy profits are in the housing market. How many people now hold the keys to Florida condominiums that they thought would keep escalating in value, only to have the bubble burst? Now they're worth a fraction of what they paid, with little hope of a quick bounce-back in the market. All those people who defaulted on home loans? They wanted more house than they could afford, and the lenders lost all discipline in the grab for profits. Those are classic characteristics of the microwave culture.

You can see the varied pitfalls of trying to microwave your way to riches and fame. Now that we've defined it and understand it, the next question is logical: How do we create success living in this culture? For starters, you've got to be extremely thick-skinned. Criticism cannot affect you to the point that you deviate from your plan. You cannot let a day's problem, or a basketball loss, allow doubt to creep in. During his tenure with the New York Yankees, Joe Torre was the best in sports at handling the microwave culture—and when you work for the Steinbrenners and live in the New York media market, you know that every defeat can be turned into a high-volume referendum on your competence. The NFL equivalent has been Tony Dungy of the Indianapolis Colts—he has the perfect temperament to handle the highs and lows of sports without overreacting. Torre and Dungy have excelled at keeping the big picture in perspective and staying focused on the long-range plan.

Pulling myself out of the microwave mindset and gaining more perspective and patience came easier for me after Billy Minardi's death. Losses were not life-and-death happenings. They didn't alter the most important things in my life: family, friends, health, and helping others. It became easier to accept the inevitable ups and downs of a season after going through 9/11.

I made my reputation by quick-fixing basketball programs, but my work at Louisville has been more of a slow-cooked success. We've now completed our seventh season here, and the program is in its best shape since the 1980s—ready to be a national contender for the foreseeable future. However, while we built for the future at Louisville, we also made some simultaneous allowances to the culture and turned that culture to our advantage. When short-term goals are met, we celebrated them as noteworthy: winning 20 games the first year and returning to postseason play, after a 12–19 record the previous season; going to the NCAA tournament the next year; advancing to the 2005 Final Four; reaching a regional final in 2008 and finishing the season in the *USA Today*/ESPN Top 10. Louisville had only one Top 10 finish in the polls in the 15 years before I arrived, so these achievements all were important.

What we're trying to do is to simultaneously develop, manage, and balance two plans. One is the long-range plan—creating goals and a strategy that go beyond what the microwave culture presents as a timetable. The other is the short-range plan—how do we win today, without rushing the process?

As famed former General Electric CEO Jack Welch once said, "You can't grow long-term if you can't eat short-term. Anybody can manage short. Anybody can manage long. Balancing those two things is what management is."

You have to have instant success, but you have to understand that it doesn't change the foundation for future success. Planning your own improvement can be a similar two-tiered approach: subtle changes and drastic changes. For the subtle, short-term approach: I'll set out to learn something new on my computer, in a day or two. For the dramatic, long-term approach: We'll improve our recruiting computer database for every prospect. You have to build it both ways, which is a tactic I have embraced.

With so many players moving on to the NBA as quickly as possible, it doesn't make sense to recruit nothing but blue-chip talent. If you bring in five prep All-Americans who leave your program for the pros after a year or two, you're in constant rebuilding mode; you've fallen victim to the microwave culture. That happened to us for a time at Louisville; several signees never even made it to campus in their rush to turn pro. We figured out that the best way to build a program today is to recruit a mixture of players: Bring in a superstar recruit or two every season, but supplement them with solid players who will be there for four years. Then you work vigilantly with those guys to improve their games. By the time they're done, they might have pro potential of their own—and they've helped you build your team along the way.

Problems arise when the four-year guys get a taste of early success and think they're two-year guys. It goes to their heads and they lose perspective. That is the microwave culture at work, too: Instant gratification comes to a young player, and he thinks he's arrived. Now all the perspiration and hard work he put into getting that success goes by the wayside. We dealt with that at Louisville in 2007 with our sophomore point guard, Edgar Sosa.

Edgar is a very emotional young man from New York who got caught up in the way he ended his freshman season, in 2006–07. He scored 47 points in two NCAA tournament games, including 31 playing against future NBA draft lottery pick Acie Law of Texas A&M. Although he made some key errors down the stretch of that game in a very close loss, Edgar was spectacular that day. We all could see his potential—but all Edgar seemed to see was his arrival as a finished product. His vision became clouded. He bought into the public and media recognition more than into our private coaching, which conveyed a more realistic message: We're proud of your progress, but you have to keep it up. Don't stop now, because there's still so much growing to do. Instead of maturely handling the praise that came his way and continuing to work on his weaknesses, Edgar regressed.

Many players enjoy a big jump in productivity from their freshman to sophomore seasons, but his numbers decreased in every major statistical category. Like many young players, he was overly concerned about his scoring. I told him that after being involved in eight NBA drafts, pro coaches, scouts, and general managers did not discuss scoring averages when evaluating players. They looked at other statistics much more closely and generally discussed a basic theme: Does this player make other people better, and would he make our team better? As a point guard that should have been Edgar's primary concern, but he wanted the instant glory of points and applause.

Meanwhile, his competition for playing time, junior Andre McGee, had not been sitting still and accepting his fate as a backup. Andre lost weight during the off-season, improving his quickness and his defense. He laced up his sneakers, came to practice, and competed—and even when Andre was not playing, his team-first attitude was evident on the bench. In contrast, Edgar often looked miserable whenever he was out of the game.

There is a noticeable difference between the two point guards in raw talent, but there was no difference between them that year in terms of productivity. Now Andre is in his senior season and has been voted a team captain. We'll see whether Edgar learns from his struggles and has stepped up his game to meet Andre's challenge. I'm convinced his junior season will be his best season to date in college, because humility has a way of bringing out the best in people. Edgar now has new perspective on how to once again be a great college basketball player.

Our other battle with the microwave culture in the last season centered around forward Earl Clark. Earl is a gifted player: a great athlete for his size (six feet nine, 225 pounds), and he's coming off a strong sophomore season. At the end of that season, it was clear that he was considering going pro, and he declared his intention to enter the NBA draft. Most scouts projected him as a first-round pick, but in the latter part of the first round. When I met with Earl to discuss his decision, I knew that pointing out the incomplete nature of his game would not get through to him. He committed seven turnovers in our regional final loss to North Carolina, some of them at absolutely key points in the game, but he knew what the projections said and that was enough for him, so I had to approach it a different way.

I pointed out that his eagerness to cash an immediate check might not be as wise as waiting a year and cashing a larger check. If he was, say, the 27th pick in the first round, he might get a $40,000-per-year shoe contract for four years. If he stayed in school, improved his game, and was drafted in the top 10, that figure could be $200,000 a year for four years. So he could take $160,000 over four years now or get $800,000 over the same time period if he waited—and the closer he is to being pro-ready when he enters the NBA, the greater the chance for a huge second contract after finishing a rookie contract that is dictated by the league's pay scale. Earl wasn't ready to buy into it on the spot, though. He needed to get away from me and think about it. When he came back, he decided to stay. "I'm not afraid of hard work, and I don't need to have the money now," he said. He made a good business decision and a good basketball decision.

The business parallel can be the eager young employee who

leaves a good long-term job for a quick monetary gain. A $30,000-per-year raise might sound great at first, but after taxes, how much is your lifestyle truly going to change? If that young employee leaves a stable company that values her contribution, is mentoring her, and gives her the opportunity for upward mobility, she might cost herself a great deal more down the road. Simply put, you can't make rash decisions based on next year's salary. You have to look further ahead than the microwave culture wants you to look.

But to compete at the highest level, in basketball or in business, coaches and CEOs have to bring in the best talent. The important part is finding gifted people who also understand the team perspective. Intelligence and talent are obvious; finding intelligent and talented people who also fit into the team concept is the real challenge.

Those doing the hiring have to understand that even most team-first stars are in a hurry to shine. They were raised in this culture and are part of this culture; don't expect them to change. The young, aggressive person in your organization might not be spoiled by success, but he is accustomed to living life at an accelerated pace.

A prime example of this for us is Samardo Samuels, a freshman on our Louisville basketball team this season. Samardo was rated among the top three high school seniors in the nation by virtually every scouting service, and some rated him No. 1. He's six feet nine, 250 pounds, gifted physically, and a tremendous competitor. He will compete for immediate playing time—and because of his success to date, he will be expecting immediate gratification. Even though he possesses a great attitude as the product of a humble upbringing—perfect team attributes—he will be in a rush to have his journey to the NBA complete in a short period of time.

Samardo has to look at two sets of goals for himself: How good can he be right away, and what will it take him to get ready for the NBA? He's good enough to play for the Louisville Cardinals right now, but he's not ready to do battle with the Kevin Garnetts, Tim Duncans, and Rasheed Wallaces of the world yet. At a young age, you can improve by leaps and bounds—but you cannot transform yourself overnight. It will take him at least a full year of incredibly hard work here at Louisville to be prepared for the NBA—if then.

I recruited Samardo, and I think he's a two-year college player at least, possibly three—but I know in his mind he's a one-year college player. Even with my pro background, I can't rely on my expertise to determine that Samardo Samuels needs two or three years of college and thus he'll stay that long before going pro. I have to assume he's planning on entering the 2009 draft.

Looking at this rationally isn't as important as looking at it from the player's point of view. The NBA is full of players who weren't ready to contribute right away—but that didn't stop them from being drafted, and thus it won't stop other young players from entering the draft before the ideal time. I have to accept that and plan for it in my recruiting. I have to be ready to sign another gifted big man this year to take Samardo's place, on the reasonable chance that he's one-and-done in college. Yes, that's a concession to the microwave culture, but if you don't make that concession, you'll no longer be competitive at the highest level. Turnover is a fact of life in today's college basketball and in today's business world. Personnel losses can lead to a downward turn for a team or a firm—to a period of doubt, a dip in productivity, a momentary crisis within an organization. Will you be ready to rebound from those personnel losses and move forward? You will be only if you've anticipated it and prepared for it by stocking up on future stars and leaders.

The dynamics are similar at the coaching level at what are called mid-major schools, and also at the CEO level of moderately sized companies. Colleges that are a step below the perennial powers are always at risk of having their talented coaches poached by the schools that can offer more money, more television exposure, more access to top players and a chance to compete for a national championship. Mid-level companies are similarly at risk of losing their rising stars to massive corporations. A hot CEO who is having a quick effect on the bottom line will attract attention.

Look at the Drake University basketball program, for example. In 2007–08, the Bulldogs had a miraculous season. A program that had not won its conference or qualified for the NCAA tournament since 1971 did both in spectacular fashion, catching lightning in a bottle and going 28–5 under their rookie head coach, Keno Davis. The son of former college coaching great Tom Davis was named the Associated Press National Coach of the Year—and he suddenly became a hot commodity in the microwave culture.

Even though he'd only proven himself for one season, Davis was snapped up by Providence College of the high-profile Big East Conference to become its next head coach. Hopefully Davis' upgrade works out, because it is a gamble. In this particular case, I think it was a worthwhile gamble by Providence. Keno Davis grew up in a basketball family and learned from his dad, who has a great basketball mind. I believe this is a great hire by the Friars, but hires such as this don't always work out. Colleges and corporations that go after the Flavor of the Month don't always like the aftertaste. Coaches' reputations can go from good to great too quickly, and they can go from bad to unbearable just as fast.

On the other end of the Davis-to-Providence move sat Drake,

suddenly without a coach. The euphoria had to dissipate quickly in Des Moines, after being burned by the microwave culture. Drake wound up hiring an assistant coach from Arizona State, Mark Phelps. He's had a decade to learn from one of the best teachers in basketball, my old assistant and current Arizona State head coach Herb Sendek, and hopefully it will work out well for him and for Drake—but Drake might now find out what life is like in the mid-major spin cycle. If the Bulldogs keep winning, bigger schools will keep coming after their coaches and it will be difficult to maintain continuity. It has happened repeatedly at Western Kentucky University, losing talented coaches Ralph Willard, Dennis Felton, and Darrin Horn to bigger programs within the last 15 years.

The only ways to maintain success during periods of high turnover are to continually attract great talent, to surround the leader with a competent staff of future leaders, and to be prepared to adapt to change. Ideally, a head coach has groomed an assistant who can step in and take his place when the offer to upgrade comes. By the same token, a company should have at least one—and preferably several—vice presidents in the succession pipeline if the CEO takes off. That's why you're not just hiring a person to take over, you're hiring a team.

Butler is the model program for building an internal pipeline that sustains itself. Barry Collier had success there in the 1990s before moving to Nebraska. When he left, Butler hired his assistant, Thad Matta, and the program stayed strong. After Matta left for Xavier and ultimately Ohio State—where he played for the 2007 national title—they handed the job to his assistant, Todd Lickliter. He took Butler to great heights, making it a weekly presence in the Top 25 in 2006–07, before leaving for Iowa after that season. Once more, Butler stayed within the family and promoted assistant Brad Stevens, who at the age of 31 guided the Bulldogs to a 30–4 record. Smart staffing has helped Butler survive this rapid turnover and given it a reputation as the college basketball cradle of coaches.

Looking outside the infrastructure, as Drake did, can also pay dividends—if the people doing the hiring are plugged in and make sound decisions. Our athletic director at Louisville, Tom Jurich, is renowned in college athletics for his ability to find rising young coaches and hire them with lightning speed. His coaching hires have resurrected our football, baseball, and track programs, among others, making them national contenders. Tom has a keen eye for talent and is never caught off-guard when a vacancy appears in his department. The joke at Louisville is that he walks around with a list in his pocket of five potential replacements for every coach at the school—and it might not be a joke. (I'm trying to get into his office to find his list of the five guys who might replace me.)

It should be the same way in business. Goldman Sachs is going to have its eyes on a dynamic trader at Merrill Lynch—and Merrill Lynch should know that. If it loses that trader, it should be prepared to poach one from somewhere else. The unintended benefit of high turnover is that talented young people will see your company as a place to get ahead and succeed, so attracting quality replacements when jobs open can be easier. Still, the bottom line is preparedness in the corner offices. CEOs who understand the microwave culture aren't caught flat-footed by sudden personnel changes. Those CEOs also understand that the demands to be successful *right now* are always there, just as they are in business. In fact, I like the way the business world is based on quarterly reports. I try to do that in basketball, breaking down our progress not by that day, but by quarters.

We have summer workouts, and our strength coaches chart the

players' work in the weight room and in various conditioning tests. They routinely check body fat to see whether our players are on task toward meeting their physiological goals. Then in the fall, we chart their performance in individual basketball workouts—how many shots do they make from each spot on the floor in a 42-minute drill? We have the season itself, which has its own obvious set of defining feedback—how many wins, how many losses? When the season is over, we have a fourth quarter of review and rehash, thoroughly examining everything we did during the season to determine what we can do better. It's not a bad way to do it.

This method breaks down your year by short gains and long gains, and then you can assess the year within the scope of your long-range plans. In basketball terms, you have to win right now with the team, and you recruit accordingly. However, you also have to realize in recruiting, if you have a very good basketball team, you could lose five or six players to the pros and you have to plan for that. You have to replace greatness with greatness, year after year, for an extended period of time.

I believe it all goes back to maintaining a consistent effort. The parts can change, but the one thing that cannot change is consistent effort on the parts of everybody in your organization. I have no problem impatiently demanding consistent effort from my players and assistant coaches—but I will not bow to impatient demands from the outside on how fast we should get things done.

Surviving the microwave culture means being able to take some heat. It also means understanding that the path to greatness is rarely easy and rarely glamorous, as we'll see in the next chapter.

## Surviving and Thriving in the Microwave Culture

**REBOUND RULES:**

✦ **Accept it.** Like the technology that fostered the microwave culture, it isn't going away and will only accelerate.

✦ **Plan two different paths to success,** short term and long term, and learn how to balance them.

✦ **Develop a thick skin.** Understand constructive criticism, but filter out the unproductive noise generated by sheer impatience.

**POINTS OF CAUTION:**

✦ **Don't panic when you lose personnel,** even when you think they're making bad decisions based on short-term impulses.

✦ **Don't lag behind the technological curve.** Be up to speed on all advances, because your competition will be. Don't give them an edge.

✦ **Don't just focus on the big score, because it won't last.** To build success, you need a lot of little scores, too.

# Chapter Five

# The Formula for Chemistry

**C**HEMISTRY IS A MAGIC INGREDIENT in successful sports teams, businesses, marriages, and almost all aspects of life. It's hard to define, but even harder to do without. Very few great things are accomplished alone, which means you must have the help of others—and tremendous team efforts are rarely accomplished without tremendous team chemistry.

It's the common denominator of teams that win and businesses that turn profits—everyone subscribing to the same common goal. It's evident in movies, when the sparks fly as two costars hit it off—Katherine Hepburn and Spencer Tracy, Elizabeth Taylor and Richard Burton, William Hurt and Kathleen Turner. It was evident watching John Stockton and Karl Malone run the pick-and-roll seamlessly, year after year, with the Utah Jazz. It's been evident for generations of fans who have watched Mick Jagger and Keith Richards make the Rolling Stones an enduring musical giant.

Virtually every successful work environment has a chemistry

that helps create camaraderie and feeds every employee's passion, but there are exceptions to the rule. The Oakland A's baseball teams of the early 1970s and the New York Yankees of the late '70s had plenty of conflicting personalities in the clubhouse, but they were able to come together long enough on the field of play to win World Series titles. Talent overcame turmoil, but that's not the norm. Much more often, chemistry is needed to create a common bond and a willingness to sacrifice for the greater good of the team. It's what teamwork is all about.

The question is whether great chemistry is created by nature or nurture. Can you build it, or does it happen on its own? My answer is a little of both. You need people with a natural proclivity for unselfishness. They care about their teammates—they get excited seeing their comrades succeed, and they hurt when they see their comrades fail. If at least some of that wasn't instilled in them at a young age, it can be difficult to create it in young adulthood. But you also can find ways to cultivate chemistry within your work force. They bring the attitude with them, and you shape it. How? With love and discipline in the right doses. With positive and negative reinforcement. And by example. Finding the right formula, with the right ingredients and elements, is the key.

The first ingredient should be a strong dose of humility. We've talked about it elsewhere in this book, but it is especially vital within a group dynamic. Humility can be a power source for an organization or it can be a power drain.

Terrell Owens' public sniping at quarterback Jeff Garcia and coach Steve Mariucci turned into a chemistry meltdown in San Francisco. Then Philadelphia took its turn with Owens, and the results were similar; another public feud with the quarterback that resulted in the talented wide receiver moving on again. The third destination was Dallas, where Owens' public preening was a very bad mix with Bill Parcells' personality. As of this writing, Owens' lack of humility has created innumerable headlines but led to zero Super Bowl rings.

Chad Johnson has been a similar power drain in Cincinnati, running his mouth repeatedly about his unhappiness with the Bengals. Even a marvelous talent like Kobe Bryant has allowed a lack of humility to mar his career.

In Kobe's situation, he did not want to be part of the Los Angeles Lakers unless they could be built to win a championship. His demands eventually led the Lakers to make a key trade that got them to the NBA Finals, but what he did to bring about that change was anything but humble. His public ranting could have instead been handled behind closed doors with the same result.

A lack of humility alienates teammates and fans—but that doesn't mean you can't entertain like Muhammad Ali and Magic Johnson. However, Magic, in particular, was about the team— even though he had a starring role and loved it with the "showtime" Lakers of the 1980s. He was a charismatic leader who knew how to stir the passion within his teammates. He was always pass before shot; always ready to celebrate the group achievements over the individual gains.

The other athletes mentioned here live on an island, not understanding what chemistry is all about. I hope that with time and maturity this will change for all three talented individuals. We'll wait and see.

After humility, we must have motivation for successful chemistry. You cannot motivate until you understand the individual motives of your players. From the outset, we realize that everyone does not react the same way to the same stimuli. Team leaders and team members alike must accept that—there are a variety of motives that drive us to work hard and strive for excellence. Some play for pride, some because of family pressure, some for monetary gain, some are simply in pursuit of excellence. You cannot push the same buttons with everyone and expect them to all respond the same way.

Before every season, I sit down with my athletes individually and communicate with them—primarily by listening. They're going to hear me talk plenty during the season, and they're going to do the majority of the listening then, so beforehand, I want to hear them articulate their goals and objectives. I want to know what they're playing for and why. What price are they willing to pay for success? What lengths will they go to in order to be extraordinary? What buttons can I push to help them get there? And, most importantly, how can we mold a collective will out of these different people who arrive with different motivations? How can we create chemistry?

We try to make it clear that none of our individual goals and motivations can be met without buying into team success and achieving team goals. I have shown our players countless times that the straightest path to individual recognition is through team accomplishments. It's been more than 50 years since the Heisman trophy winner came from a losing team; they come from teams in the hunt for the national title in college football. In basketball, they don't just select the top scorers for the All-America team— they take the best players from the teams that are having the most success. Winning games always trumps individual statistics when it comes to gaining glory. If your players embrace that, it's so much easier to blend individual egos into a team ego.

Rewarding team-first behavior cannot be stressed often enough. In fact, it should be a daily habit that starts with the boss. If you want your message to be delivered correctly and with maximum impact, deliver it yourself. Do your own talking. Be your own messenger.

That's why I verbally reinforce the great pass in every practice. When we watch film, I point out the unselfish ball movement that creates an open shot. When a player helps out on defense by taking a charge, that deserves an enthusiastic response from the coaches. Reinforce exactly what you want when you see your people doing it. When someone dives for a loose ball or hustles from one end of the floor to the other to deflect a pass, we want everyone on the bench cheering. It's got to become a culture within your team, an ethos that informs everything you do. The New England Patriots have done great work building that no-ego culture in the NFL, and their tremendous records in recent years are no coincidence. The undefeated team the Patriots chased in 2007, the 1972 Miami Dolphins, was led by a unit called the No-Name Defense. They really were the No-Ego Defense, unconcerned with who got the credit as long as the Dolphins got the win. That defense was an example of chemistry being enhanced from within the work force.

The head coach of a team or the CEO of a company cannot spend her entire workday making sure her players or employees get along and care about each other—much of that has to come from your team leaders. There will be inevitable disputes and disagreements among those people—if you saw the bickering that went on in *The Apprentice* when Donald Trump was out of the room, you know what I mean—but they cannot be allowed to proliferate and poison the atmosphere. They won't if your internal leadership is strong. If the most experienced people in your locker room or in your office cubicles are positive, team-first people who set a great example for others to follow, everyone should flourish. To cite the Patriots again, that's what Tom Brady brings to their locker room. He's as big a star as there is in the NFL, but he does not carry himself like a superstar around his peers—and they follow his lead. Even Randy Moss, a wide receiver with a reputation for being a problematic teammate, fell in line quickly with tremendous results.

Disagreements will be short-lived and overwhelmed by an aura of unity. Peer-driven chemistry is essential to success. That's why recruiting with an eye on how each person might affect group dynamics—whether it's players or workers—is vitally important. But just as a single individual can positively affect chemistry, so too can a single individual negatively impact a team. Positive attitudes inflate and elevate your team's balloon, while negative attitudes suck the air right out.

That's why, when I'm recruiting a high school player, I don't just watch how he plays. I watch how he responds to coaching, and how he responds to his teammates when he's out of the game. Is he listening when the coaches offer feedback, or is he staring in the other direction? Is he cheering for his teammates, or has he checked out emotionally because his stats can't get any better on the bench? Most high-school stars will not be as successful in college—that's just the nature of the beast as the level of play increases. Young men who averaged 25 points per game become role players, earning only a fraction of the playing time and adulation they were accustomed to at a lower level. It's important to have players who avoid turning bitter as their roles diminish. A guy who averages two points per game can still make a big impact in the locker room—sometimes negatively. A coach needs to communicate with his 10th, 11th, and 12th players as effectively as he does with his stars to make sure they understand their value to the team.

In the early 1990s, we were building the foundation of greatness at the University of Kentucky. We brought in one successful recruiting class after another, pushing our talent base to new levels of excellence, but to reach national championship caliber, we had to take a gamble on a talented, six-foot–eight forward from Chicago named Antoine Walker. He was a McDonald's All-American who arrived with an outsized ego, having lived in a world of instant gratification. He had spent years with people who paid close attention to his points and "touches"—the number of times he touched the ball on offense. He was going to be high maintenance.

Antoine's freshman season of 1994–95 was filled with discipline issues, early-morning running sessions, and constant reinforcement of team objectives over his individual numbers. His older teammates were often turned off by a temperamental freshman who didn't think he needed to wait his turn before becoming a star. At times, I wondered whether this difficult undertaking would be worth it in the long run.

As it turned out, Antoine was worth every challenging moment. Why? He produced, and wound up doing it within the team concept. He ended his freshman season on a high note, being named Most Outstanding Player of the Southeastern Conference tournament as we upset defending national champion Arkansas. As a sophomore, he helped lead us to the national championship as our second-leading scorer, top rebounder, and No. 2 assists leader. After that season, he turned pro and was taken with the No. 6 pick in the 1996 NBA draft.

We got through to Antoine by recognizing what motivated him: playing time, scoring, and attention. I understood that we weren't going to dramatically change him; we just had to get him to take good shots and to accept that the spotlight would find him through winning. I lavished praise on him for his passing, trying to reinforce that team-first behavior, and telling him that made his star shine brighter than anyone else's on our very talented team. His motives didn't change, but his path to success did. Without Antoine on board, we wouldn't have been one of the most dominant teams in college basketball history.

I also had two other tools at my disposal for dealing with Antoine: great upper-class leadership on the team, and great competition for playing time. Seniors Tony Delk, Walter McCarty, and Mark Pope, and junior Derek Anderson weren't going to let one questionable attitude sour the locker room. They kept Antoine in his place and led by example—exactly the kind of peer pressure you need within your workforce. It's more important to establish your leadership behind closed doors than in a public forum. We had solid people there to take charge in the coaches' absence.

But competing for your job is the best motivator of all. On that 1995–96 Kentucky team, we had eight future NBA players. Antoine Walker was tremendously talented, but he wasn't irreplaceable—and I replaced him often when he lapsed into me-first basketball. The bench is a valuable motivator, especially when it's used on someone who just loves to play. Antoine was a true basketball junkie, always looking for a game out of season. In season, I knew how much he hungered to be on the court every minute. That's why I sat him down for the last 18 minutes of the '96 SEC tournament championship game against Mississippi State. We lost in shocking fashion, and a lot of people said I "threw" that game by keeping Antoine out for that long. Honestly, winning that game was far less important than delivering a lesson that stuck with Antoine through our NCAA tournament run: Play the right way or don't play at all. He got his head straight after that, and we didn't lose again that year.

I had an even bigger turnaround at Louisville with a young man named Ellis Myles. In the course of three years, Ellis went from a major chemistry detriment to a major chemistry attribute. It was one of the most profound attitude adjustments I've seen in all my years as a coach.

In March 2001, after being introduced as the new coach of the Cardinals at the Louisville Convention Center and shaking hands with hundreds of people, I had the distinct pleasure of meeting a group of athletes who turned my stomach: my new team. I had heard some horror stories: They had verbally abused their aging, Hall of Fame coach, Denny Crum, talking back to him on the bench and during timeouts. I couldn't believe the stories, because this was one of the least-talented teams in Louisville history—they'd gone 12–19 that season, forcing Crum's retirement. What they lacked in talent, they made up for in bad attitude—and no matter what you hear about the NBA, where I had just been, that sort of disrespect of a coach did not occur. That incident of Latrell Sprewell choking P. J. Carlesimo was the rare exception, certainly not the rule.

When I entered the room with these players, I went around introducing myself. The players all smiled and shook my hand. After the fifth player, I blurted out a vulgarity and stopped; not a single player had told me his name. "You guys must think I spent all winter watching you play," I said. "But I was kind of busy try-ing to stop Kobe Bryant and Tim Duncan and Allen Iverson, so I didn't catch the names of your sorry asses. So it might be helpful if you introduced yourself and let me know your names, at least for the two weeks before I throw you off the team." They were stunned, and many of them were immediately scared straight—but not the incumbent starting power forward.

When we started doing individual-instruction workouts with the players that spring, I came across an attitude more corrosive than Antoine Walker's. It belonged to Ellis Myles. He was a six-foot-eight, 260-pounder from Compton, California, in lousy shape and packing a surly demeanor. Within 10 minutes of his first workout, he and I arrived at a crossroads. When he didn't put forth maximum effort in our opening drills, I lit into him as hard as any player I've coached. I asked him to cite what he had accomplished during his freshman season on a 12–19 team. And, I said, when you've covered those high points in 10 seconds, tell me about what you accomplished in high school. That should take another 20 seconds.

"So you have 30 seconds to change your attitude," I told Ellis, "or I'm putting you on a bus back to Compton." He started crying. To see this tough guy from Compton in tears was something to behold. I told him to go to my office and we'd settle this.

I informed Ellis that he was straddling a fence. On one side was the opportunity to turn around his life. On the other is the chance to throw away a basketball career, a scholarship, and a college education. I told him to find his motivation and discover his passion, or he was through as a Cardinal. I gave him a list of goals he had to meet by the end of the summer to stay on the team: He had to cut his body fat percentage in half, from 20 percent to less than 10; he had to maintain perfect class attendance; he had to give maximum effort in every individual instruction; and he had to show respect to everyone on the staff.

Ellis wound up changing dramatically. He lost the weight and became a savvy, tough, on-court leader of our 2005 Final Four team—an average-to-good team that overachieved in part because of great chemistry. There were times during his college career when I still needed to give him a one-on-one attitude adjustment, but he always responded. During that Final Four year, *Sports Illustrated*'s Seth Davis listed a group of "Glue Guys" in college basketball who did the little things to make a team a winner. None other than Ellis Myles was on the list, having somehow gone from a guy who could tear a team apart to someone who could hold it together. He's currently on my staff as an assistant strength coach, with aspirations to become a full-time assistant.

Unfortunately, not every player story ends as successfully as Antoine's or Ellis'. I won't go into specific names—who is not as important as why when it comes to understanding what detracts from a group undertaking—but I have coached individuals who single-handedly damaged team chemistry to the point that I had to dismiss them.

You're not going to get every personnel decision right, in hiring or recruiting. Mistakes in judgment are made. To minimize them when putting together a team, in sports or business, you have to listen to delve into the psyche of your people. In doing that, you might be able to recognize the eight traits that can corrupt chemistry:

1. **Jealousy.** It's a surefire way to disrupt the unity of any team. We must instill a belief with all our team members that everyone succeeds when one of us succeeds. There should be a sense of satisfaction from watching someone else excel, knowing that we all had

a hand in it. It certainly helps when the stars are humble and remember to recognize their cohorts when receiving awards or honors—but even if they don't, the mindset should be that what's good for one is good for all.

How to prevent jealousy: Work hard to disburse credit equally among your constituents. You should have a well-honed sense of fairness and be sharply attuned to who isn't feeling the appropriate amount of love. Little ego strokes can make a big difference. Use examples of destructively jealous behavior that can serve as a deterrent. I told my Louisville team about a player with the 1987–88 Knicks who resented the attention being given to a younger teammate. I told my current players, "Can you believe someone would have their vision so clouded that they couldn't see the recognition they all were getting from their team success?" Create a sense of embarrassment for anyone who might subscribe to those feelings. Let them think, "That could be me they're poking fun of if I don't change my ways."

Iron out all differences right away by getting those at odds together to talk it out. Let nothing fester. Communication is vital.

Know and understand your team members. Those with low self-esteem must be watched closely to make sure they don't fall into the ranks of the jealous. Help them establish their own identity.

2. **Cynicism.** It will infiltrate when the going gets tough. Cynical people believe they are not part of the problem. Cynical people question the plan and doubt the leader. That's because cynical people don't understand how to find the proper solutions to the problem. In

their minds, the end result will not be positive, so they're not going to fully commit to the group effort.

How to prevent cynicism: A one-on-one meeting that confronts the cynical individual with his own behavior is a must. Most negative people don't realize how they're tearing apart the fiber of a team unless it's pointed out to them. Leave no doubt that the cynical behavior must change. There will be consequences for anything that undermines team chemistry.

Create a plan for how to change that behavior, and create checkpoints to monitor that person's progress. In basketball terms, is the cynical player on his feet and applauding for teammates during games when he's not playing? Is he the first player on the spot to offer a hand to a teammate who has been knocked down? Is he on time for every practice? The videotape and the clock on the wall will provide objective answers to those questions. In business, punctuality can be monitored, as well as an employee's willingness to speak up and interact in meetings.

(As an aside: I also find the growing trend of securing verbal scholarship commitments from eighth-graders and ninth-graders to be a cynical practice. There is very little sincerity in it. Coaches and prospects are free to do as they wish, but I can assure you it's nothing more than a publicity stunt. A talented eighth-grader who is being wooed in this fashion stands a chance of losing perspective, losing his work ethic, and developing one of those attitudes that kills team chemistry. The cynical part is the lack of any real commitment on either side; what validity does it have? It's like meeting someone at age 14 and saying, "I'd like for us to get engaged and married at 21." It may happen, but I don't like the odds.)

3. **Inflated ego.** It occurs when team members believe the group cannot function or succeed without them, because they're so far superior to their cohorts. Even the most talented individuals in any endeavor must realize that their value only matters within the framework of the group.

A cleanup hitter has to value the hitters who get on base before him. He must recognize that his RBI total is dependent upon those base runners, who allow him to create big moments. A person with an inflated ego prevents others from reaching their potential by demanding the spotlight, while simultaneously overestimating his own abilities. His potential often goes unmet because too much emotion has been invested on self-appeasement.

How to prevent inflated ego: Make sure the egotistical team member is aware of the talents of those around him, and encourage him to recognize those while checking his own ego at the door. Point out to that person that there is room for improvement in his performance; believe it or not, they're not perfect. Keeping them humble and working to improve every day is vital. In many recovery programs, ego is said to stand for "Edging God Out." It might be worth reminding the egotistical that only the Almighty is immune to self-improvement.

Ignore false praise and instant gratification. If your egotistical worker cannot differentiate false praise from legitimate praise, point it out to her. Along the way, help that person enjoy the fruits of other people's labor. Openly celebrate the collective success yourself and it will set an example for everyone else to follow.

4. **Inflexible personality.** "I know I'm right. You just don't understand. I can't believe you don't see it that

way." Sound familiar? You've probably heard some of that in your office. The inflexible personality does far more talking than listening, like one of those TV talk shows that put four pundits in boxes and have them try to outshout each other. The inflexible personality can find fault with others but rarely himself—embellishing points and stories to portray others as unreasonable. The inflexible personality will argue against every criticism of his performance, no matter how small. Unfortunately for that person, there are no guarantees that his way is the only way.

In a productivity race, a stubborn person often is running in ankle weights, slowing themselves down through obstinacy. When I'm faced with a suggestion that doesn't fit my strategy, I might sidestep the argument by saying, "I like it. We can possibly use it down the road, if not right now"; or, "Let's tinker with it and see if we can make it better." Flexible people understand how to communicate and understand how compromise can be crucial to accomplishing things in a timely manner. They comprehend the goal and make things happen to reach that goal, even if it means compromising along the way. Being able to adjust stimulates creativity and enhances team chemistry.

How to prevent the inflexible personality: Use examples of how teams win with a variety of strategies; how they change and adapt to sustain success. The New England Patriots began their championship run with defense, but their undefeated regular season of 2007 was marked by record-breaking offense. The defensive leaders like Tedy Bruschi, Mike Vrabel, and Rodney Harrison were fine with that, as long as it was good for the group as a whole.

Challenge people to create outside their box. Don't let them sit within their comfort zone all the time, or you're limiting their growth and the growth of the group. A one-trick pony can out-live its usefulness or become outdated.

Work on agreeing and sharing. Turn disagreements into com-promises that leave all parties feeling satisfied, or at least feeling like their side was heard. Don't tolerate meetings that turn into bitchfests; they're unproductive and breed bad feelings.

5. **Discipline deficiency.** A lack of discipline leads to poor habits, and poor habits become destructive to the will of any business or team. People who are on time will notice those who are late and wonder why that behavior is tolerated. They'll think you're playing favorites. Or, the punctual people start running late as well, figuring there is no accountability for it. Sud-denly, you've got a breakdown in discipline. Morale has eroded, cynicism has crept in, and everyone is looking for shortcuts when shortcuts won't work.

Part of great chemistry is a set of rules and regulations that enhance discipline and are followed by everyone. Certainly, there are situations in which human error must be dealt with on a case-by-case basis and judgment must be exercised—you cannot be completely inflexible or overly draconian in enforcing the rules, especially when dealing with young people. But consis-tency is key, and the simpler your rules, the better. Don't leave any doubt as to where you stand.

How to prevent discipline deficiency: Stay focused on what it takes to succeed, emphasizing daily habits. Only allow deviations from those habits when it cannot be helped.

Be early and be eager to win. In Louisville basketball, fifteen minutes early is considered on time. Players straggling onto the practice court in the nick of time with their shoes untied are in for a long day of running. Develop your discipline to maximize your mental and physical health. Good habits include the way you eat, sleep, and exercise. Do those things right, do them productively, and you'll feel better about yourself. The better you feel, the more productive you'll be.

6. **Lack of passion.** If you cannot sense the energy and excitement from people you're trying to recruit or hire, they might not have it. They should be passionate and driven enough to know what they want—to have goals and expectations and to articulate what they'll do to meet them. One year I asked one of my players what he wanted to accomplish outside of basketball. This player, at the end of his junior year, responded, "I don't know." I dismissed him from my office and told him to come back the next day with something better. I told him I don't deal with I-don't-know people. At age 22, young people should have some plans and ideas, or at least be searching for help in creating them. I-don't-know people wallow in mediocrity.

People lacking passion don't enthusiastically seize every opportunity to improve themselves. They love what success could bring them, but they don't want to put in the hard work it takes to become successful. I've been lucky to coach many who were just the opposite—young men with a great passion for learning and winning within the team concept. Today, I see a player from my days at Boston University, Brett Brown, as an assistant coach with the

San Antonio Spurs. I see a guy we drafted late in the first round with the Knicks, Mark Jackson, who I'm sure will be a successful NBA coach. I see Billy Donovan winning national titles at Florida. I see Francisco Garcia playing well with the Sacramento Kings of the NBA. Their common denominator is great passion for the game.

How to prevent a lack of passion: Make your own passion a beacon for others to follow and emulate. If you're not boiling with observable enthusiasm, those around you might not, either. Try to surround yourself with high achievers. That doesn't mean you can't take a chance on a few people who haven't yet tapped into their passion, but you must believe that it's within them first. It's hard to create passion where there is none.

Celebrate the grind. When hard work yields results, point it out—loudly, if necessary. During the long hours, remind your people that it will pay off in the end—cheerfully, if possible. Tell them that the reward is in the rugged journey as much as the glorious destination—adamantly, if need be.

7.  **Excuse making.** When something goes wrong, it's never their fault. They'll point fingers in all directions except at the person in the mirror. College basketball players will blame teachers for shortcomings in the classroom, referees for bad calls, teammates for not getting them the ball. I always tell my guys that failure is OK if they own up to it and use it as fertilizer to make things better. I tell them excuses are a sign of weakness, and weakness won't be tolerated.

How to prevent excuse making: That's an easy one—don't make any yourself. Let the scoreboard and the bottom line be the judge, without rationalizing how it doesn't tell the true story. Channeling Bill Parcells once again: You are your record. In the wake of disappointment or defeat, the first finger should point at yourself. How can I improve my performance? Let everyone around you know that you're starting there, and tell them what you'll do better next time. That should inhibit the blame game from getting started.

8. **Front-running.** The front-runners are at their best when everything is going their way. It's easy to be upbeat and positive when you're playing well and your team is winning—but how do you respond when times aren't so good? Sports and business are full of people who can ride a wave of positive momentum, but aren't so good when they have to generate momentum in the face of opposition or adversity. They tire mentally and physically and are bypassed by their competition. They become self-satisfied too easily.

How to prevent front-running: Keep the hammer down during good times. My halftime speeches are always more volatile and demanding when we're ahead—players will take criticism more easily in that setting, and they'll stay on task. When we're behind, I try to be more analytical, calm, and upbeat. When we have a double-digit lead late in games, I'll tell my team during timeouts that the scoreboard doesn't matter; we're tied, and I want to win the next four minutes by the next media timeout. I create a game within a game, trying to keep the pressure on them to rely on their fundamentals and do what we've coached them to do.

Keep your own emotions on an even keel, and maintain your

discipline. If you get overly comfortable when things are going well, it's a signal to others to let their guard down and relax.

Those are the eight traits that can commonly ruin your chemistry formula. To counterbalance them, remember what makes the formula work: care and discipline; a willingness to share and sacrifice for the greater good; and a positive view of our common goals.

When those factors outweigh the negatives, and the positives come together, you create a powerful chemistry. Add passion, hunger, and drive to the equation and watch the overflowing result.

## The Formula for Chemistry

**REBOUND RULES:**

✦ **Understand what creates good chemistry—find out what's inside your workers first, and then do everything you can to motivate them.** It's part nature and part nurture.

✦ **Preach the virtues of team gain.** Illustrate the fact that ancillary individual benefits are acquired when the group wins. Never miss an opportunity to drive that home, and try to live it so those you're leading can see it.

✦ **Make sure your team leaders provide positive peer pressure to accentuate good chemistry.** It should start from the top, but it's even better if the rank and file are encouraging each other to work together.

**POINTS OF CAUTION:**

✦ **Don't let cynicism and moodiness proliferate.** They'll deflate your team in a heartbeat. If you see evidence of it, confront it and stamp it out.

✦ **Don't point fingers.** Playing the blame game in tough times is a prescription for failure and a surefire way to create divisions.

✦ **Don't be afraid of trial and error.** Tinker where you think you need it. Don't expect immediate results, either. Be willing to wait for relationships to evolve and strengthen, with your encouragement along the way.

Chapter Six

# *Achieving Greatness*

RHETORICAL INFLATION—otherwise known as hyper-bole—has cheapened the use of the word "great." Too many things are cavalierly and irresponsibly labeled "great" when "very good" or "good" would be more accurate. Real greatness is a rare thing, and should be appreciated as such.

For example, I've coached many very good college basketball teams—thirteen NCAA tournament qualifiers, nine that won a conference championship of some kind, and five that reached the ultimate destination of the Final Four—but I can count the great ones on three fingers: the 1987 Providence team that massively overachieved to reach the Final Four, the dominant 1996 Kentucky team that won the national championship, and the resilient '97 Kentucky team that narrowly missed making it a repeat.

Similarly, true greatness is hard to find in business. In the retail world, I'd classify Target as great. Their leaders have a clear under-standing of what they stand for, and they have communicated that to their customers with their simple but powerful slogan: "Expect more. Pay less." Their bull's-eye logo has become almost as recognizable a brand as the Nike swoosh, and they now have about 1,500 U.S. stores in 47 states. Target has taken the low-price shopping experience and made it chic, partnering with famous designers to create things that look good and feel good. The company has convinced customers they can get good deals without settling for the cheap quality most people associate with bargain shopping. Bottom line, Target made its customers feel smart.

Few companies have been able to get the formula exactly right and keep it right. You've heard of the book, *Good to Great*? There are many cautionary tales of going from great to good in business. America Online was supposed to be great, but it wound up forfeiting much of its early edge in the nascent Internet industry. Ford has been a powerful name in American commerce for about a century and had long stretches of greatness, but it and General Motors were outflanked by foreign automakers in the 1970s and have never fully recovered to the level of great. Shearson Lehman Brothers bought E. F. Hutton in the late 1980s for $1 billion, thinking the name would add greatness to its cachet; instead, it wound up dropping that 10-figure name several years later.

Several restaurant chains have aimed at greatness—or at least hugeness—only to find that they overextended themselves into mere goodness—or perhaps mediocrity. Darden Restaurants, Inc., bills itself as the largest full-service restaurant chain in the world—but when the company diversified far beyond its linchpin offerings of Red Lobster and Olive Garden, some of the new ideas were not as productive. China Coast, a 51-outlet Chinese food restaurant, failed in 1995. Smokey Bones, a barbecue chain, was sold off in December 2007. The Bahama Breeze chain hasn't performed well either.

Outback Steakhouse, Inc., has gone through a similar course correction. After bloating itself with Carrabba's Italian Grill, Fleming's Prime Steakhouse, Bonefish Grill, and Roy's Restaurants—and losing some of its identity—it is now in the process of undiluting its brand and making a comeback run at greatness.

Xerox had such a monopoly on the early copying industry that its name became a verb: Nobody copied documents; they "Xeroxed" them. People still said that even as they started using competitors' equipment more and more often. Xerox has made a comeback this decade, but its greatest days probably are in its rearview mirror.

But even if true greatness is difficult to achieve and sustain, we should still strive for it. Isn't it so much better to be striving for greatness than aspiring to be average? Wouldn't life become boring if we settled where we are and quit trying to challenge ourselves?

If you ask a young person why they want to be great, they may come up with material reasons: a nice car, a nice home, nice clothes. The humble, more mature person says it's not about the clothes I wear, the car I drive, or the home I live in—it's because I can affect the lives of other people in a positive way. I can watch them enjoy happiness, see them grow, and improve themselves. That's where you can achieve a sense of power, which I define as an ability to act. If you have power, you have an ability to do things for the betterment of those around you. The power to act the right way is the key, and it's a key to successful leadership.

I wanted to achieve greatness as a college athlete but had to settle for being an integral part of a team. I was a high-scoring guard in high school on Long Island, New York, but that same statistical success did not carry over to my college career at

Massachusetts. What I learned at UMass was valuable in terms of understanding the concepts of teamwork. When my four-year career was over, I had learned more than I could have imagined about the game from a mental and emotional standpoint, as opposed to just viewing it through the prism of points, assists, and rebounds. I was satisfied with my self-esteem because I made the attempt.

Now I'm trying to achieve greatness as the leader of a team. Group success is what spurs me, and what spurs most business leaders as well. We're driven to build a team ego and create a talent base that your competitors do not have. You must get your individuals to perform collectively at levels they didn't think they could attain.

Setting the bar seemingly out of reach, then watching your team surpass it—that, to me, is achieving greatness.

Of course, the individual members of your team must buy into that and strive to do the same thing in their personal careers. Some of the players I've coached have gone on to become far more successful than anyone believed possible. Nobody looked at Nazr Mohammed as a future 10-year NBA player when I recruited him to Kentucky in 1995. I remember coming into a gym in Chicago to watch him and being greeted by a high school coach who asked, "What are you doing here?"

"I'm here to see Nazr Mohammed," I told him.

"You're in the wrong gym," the coach said, pointing me toward two more highly touted Chicago-area players on another court.

We pursued him anyway, even though our main competition to sign the overweight center was from the University of Illinois–Chicago—not exactly like battling North Carolina for a McDonald's All-American. We signed Nazr, but he was a project. As a 305-pound freshman at Kentucky, he played on the junior varsity team because he was so far away from being ready to contribute to a top-ranked team.

With constant oversight and encouragement from our staff, Nazr remade his body the next year—losing 50 pounds and dropping his body fat percentage from 21 to less than 10. With his increased stamina and agility, the rest of his talents were magnified; he had tremendous hands and a wonderful touch shooting the ball. He became a key player on my last Kentucky team, which reached the 1997 national title game, and the following year he was the No. 2 scorer when the Wildcats won the national title. He entered the draft after that season, was a first-round pick, and earned an NBA championship ring in 2005. He's still making a great living playing in the league.

How did Nazr Mohammed achieve so much, when so little was expected of him? Through incredibly hard, focused work. Aside from his genetic gift of size, Nazr's career was earned and not given. That's the great news about achieving greatness: It's not all natural. You're not destined for greatness. You work your way toward it. I once wrote a book entitled *Born to Coach*, but I now realize that title is a fallacy. The world is not full of born successes, and the corner offices are not full of born business leaders. Effort can take you past the point where native talent stops.

I read a fascinating story by Geoffrey Colvin in *Money* in October of 2006. It showed, citing a variety of scientific studies, that a lack of God-given aptitude or ability does not necessarily preclude you from achieving greatness in a given field. Not even people we think of as "naturals"—musical or athletic prodigies at young ages—were simply encoded with brilliance in those certain fields.

"It's not so simple," wrote *Money*'s Colvin. "For one thing, you do not possess a natural gift for a certain job, because targeted natural gifts don't exist. . . . You are not a born CEO or investor or chess grandmaster. You will achieve greatness only through an enormous amount of hard work over many years. And not just any hard work, but work of a particular type that's demanding and painful."

He continued, "[Warren] Buffett, for instance, is famed for his discipline and the hours he spends studying financial statements of potential investment targets. The good news is that your lack of a natural gift is irrelevant—talent has little or nothing to do with greatness. You can make yourself into any number of things, and you can even make yourself great."

How do you do that? With practice, of course—but it requires practicing with perfection in mind. "Deliberate practice" is the term researchers use. Deliberate practice is focused, intense, and goal oriented. It's about setting objectives to improve every practice and charting your progress (or lack of it). Then you examine the data from your practice, get feedback from coaches or mentors, and go do it again—and again and again and again. This is where sweat equity enters the picture, but it's about more than just trying hard.

Many people today are willing to pay the price to be great; they just don't go about it the right way. That's why the example *Money* uses is a good one: "Simply hitting a bucket of balls is not deliberate practice, which is why most golfers don't get better. Hitting an eight-iron 300 times with a goal of leaving the ball within 20 feet of the pin 80 percent of the time, continually observing results and making appropriate adjustments, and doing that for hours every day—that's deliberate practice."

At Louisville, we pattern our individual instruction workouts in a similar manner. We don't just send guys into the gym to hoist a few hundred jump shots. If players were left to their unsupervised devices, too many of them would gravitate to the perimeter and jack up three-point shots without much thought put into the exercise. Three-pointers are more fun and worth more points, and so many of today's players only want to work on what's fun. That's why the loss of the mid-range game is an epidemic in college basketball—very few players take the time to deliberately practice the nuances, moves, and finesse needed to shake a defender and score in that no-man's land between the dunk and the 20-foot jumper. Ambidextrous dribbling, controlling your body, avoiding contact, and developing touch are vanishing arts.

In our individual instruction sessions, we focus on improving specific areas of performance. We stress efficiency, because wasting time is a threat to the productivity of all athletes and all businesspeople. You want to organize your time so you're getting things accomplished. So many people waste valuable time that could be going toward achieving greatness. In those 42-minute individual instructions, players go through specific shooting drills from different spots on the floor, with a manager charting the results and a coach on hand to observe and critique. They shoot the kind of shots we expect them to take (and make) during games. This is concentrated effort designed to increase skill and stamina, and to perform under physical stress.

At the end of a workout, a player has competed to reach a specific goal and can understand where he excelled and where he struggled. We compare the data to his previous workouts to see whether he's improving. We provide constant feedback on shooting form and other techniques. We set progressively higher goals and strive to reach them every day.

That is deliberate practice, and it pays off when you enter a game. If you've done everything you can to be the best you can be—whether it's weight training, conditioning, or diet—you've set the stage. If you shortchanged yourself anywhere along the way, you're not going to achieve greatness, and you've left yourself vulnerable to a lifetime of regret for squandering your potential.

I can't think of any artist who has done more deliberate practicing to be great at his craft than actor Robert DeNiro. He didn't just take on roles; he lived them. DeNiro worked as a cab driver for three months to prepare for one of his early great roles, as the sociopath Travis Bickle in *Taxi Driver*. He gained 60 pounds and learned how to box to play Jake LaMotta in *Raging Bull*. He lived in Sicily to ready himself for *The Godfather: Part II*. Those all are examples of practicing with an obvious goal in mind, and going far beyond simply honing a preexisting talent.

Jerry Rice became the greatest wide receiver in football history not because he was faster than everyone else—in fact, his draft stock dropped for the very reason that his 4.5-second time in the 40-yard dash did not dazzle the professional scouts—but no one who ever played that position has worked as hard as Rice did at preparing his body for the rigors of pro football. Read this 1998 *Outside Magazine* description of Rice's off-season workout regimen and you'll understand why he was a productive player into his 40s—an ancient age for an NFL receiver:

Rice's six-day-a-week workout is divided into two parts: two hours of cardiovascular work in the morning and three hours of strength training each afternoon. Early in the off-season, the a.m. segment consists of a five-mile trail run near San Carlos on a torturous course called, simply, The Hill. But since five vertical miles can hardly be considered a workout, he pauses on the steepest section to do a series of

ten 40-meter uphill sprints. As the season approaches, however, Rice knows it's time to start conserving energy—so
he forgoes The Hill and instead merely does a couple of
sprints: six 100-yarders, six 80s, six 60s, six 40s, six 20s, and
16 tens, with no rest between sprints and just two and a half
minutes between sets.

For the p.m. sessions he alternates between upper-body
and lower-body days. But no matter which half of his body
he's working on, the volume is always the same: three sets of
ten reps of 21 different exercises. Yes, your calculator's right:
That's 630 repetitions a day.

So Rice is the king of receivers when it came to putting in deliberate physical practice. The king of deliberate mental practice?
It has to be Raymond Berry, who had a Hall of Fame career with
the Baltimore Colts. In April 2008, *Sports Illustrated* ran an excerpt
from Mark Bowden's book, *The Best Game Ever*, a recounting of
the Colts' 1958 NFL Championship victory over the New York
Giants. The excerpt profiled Berry, whose methods of practice at
his high-school stadium in Paris, Texas, were fascinating:

> There he would set a piece of paper down on the grass and,
> for an hour or more, race off carrying a football in one di-
> rection or another, stop, return, catch his breath, consult the
> paper, assume a set position and sprint off again. Sometimes
> he would angle off to the left for a short distance, sometimes
> to the right. Sometimes he would stop and turn back a few
> steps, or perform a shuffle that looked like little dance moves
> before abruptly changing direction. Sometimes he would
> run only 10 yards and sometimes the length of the field before
> he came back. There didn't seem to be any pattern to it, so

it would have been hard for anyone to guess that the young man was playing an entire football game at the split end position in pantomime.

He had chosen the film of a particular game, observed each route run by the wide receiver, timed each play and interval between plays with a stopwatch and, in tiny, meticulous handwriting, sketched the patterns and noted the sequences. Every play, whether the receiver was thrown the ball or not; every huddle; every timeout; every stretch the wideout spent on the bench between offensive series. Then, consulting this handwritten script out on the grass, he acted out the game from whistle to whistle. Out on the playing field of his hometown in the dead of summer, there was no one to observe his obsessive devotion, no teammate, no neighbor, no coach. There was no one he was trying to impress. It was pure desire. No, not just desire. The young man in gray sweats and glasses was desperate.

After reading those examples, you're probably left with a logical question: How do you "practice" for greatness in business? As noted in the *Money* article, there are many specific ways to improve your work: rehearsing presentations; testing negotiating tactics in dry runs with fellow workers; quizzing yourself on new methods and developing trends within your field; and creating habits that force you out of your office and away from your computer screen to interact with coworkers and clients.

Many successful business people will also tell you that they're insatiable information junkies. Goldman Sachs is renowned for its data mining—sending its researchers out to extensively study consumer habits in a certain area (say, moviegoers) and then dumping that information into a database that might reveal significant trends. That agility and intelligence is one reason why they stay ahead of their competition. A current working knowledge of your industry—who's coming up, who's fading, who's resting on their laurels, where the business is headed—is a significant part of practicing to succeed. To gain that knowledge, you must be intrigued and fascinated by the subject matter—for example, if you work on Wall Street, your eyes dilate when there's a significant fluctuation in the Hong Kong market.

But here is the most difficult part of achieving greatness: It can take years of that sort of backbreaking effort. Of course, that is at odds with the microwave culture discussed in a previous chapter—we are conditioned to expect immediate results and immediate gratification. Deliberate practice produces results quickly, but taking that all the way to greatness is a long haul. Even the most accomplished humans generally needed a decade of intense training to reach an elite level. Researchers refer to it as the "10-year rule." Yes, it can take an entire decade of devoted practice to attain mastery of a given pursuit—and that doesn't really jive with the microwave culture timetable, does it?

Tiger Woods was a golf prodigy, hitting balls with astonishing ability on the *Mike Douglas Show* as a toddler, but it was his continued hard work, under the relentless tutelage of his father, Earl, that transformed him from a precocious talent into the best golfer in the world. Even after reaching the summit of his sport, Woods has continued his efforts to improve, significantly retooling his swing on a couple of occasions. If his putting stroke gets shaky, he will hit hundreds of five-footers until his confidence is restored. If he's momentarily lost confidence off the tee, he'll hit balls for hours to regain it. Refusing to settle for superiority when there is still room for improvement—that's the sign of someone absolutely determined to achieve greatness.

*Money* cites chess champion Bobby Fischer, who became a grandmaster at age 16. He was a natural, right? No. He'd been immersed in chess instruction for nine years before reaching that level. The magazine also cited a study by Florida State University professor K. Anders Ericsson that found that practice time and achievement are inseparable. Ericsson studied 20-year-old violinists and found that the best group, as judged by conservatory teachers, averaged 10,000 hours of deliberate practice in their lives. The next best average 7,500 hours and the next 5,000.

In all walks of life, thorough preparation is vital when performing under pressure. I've always said pressure is your ally; it is your best friend. When you've done the work to get ready and then you apply pressure to yourself, it brings out the best in you in every step along the way. That's the positive momentum that spurs you to excel.

In the heat of a close game, a basketball coach with thorough knowledge of his opponent and his own players will know what weakness he can exploit when drawing up a last-second play. A musician who has practiced her solo thousands of times will be comfortable when the curtain goes up in Carnegie Hall. A salesman who has relentlessly honed his pitch will be confident in closing deals during the final weeks of a sales quarter. They all will feel a sense of calmness even at stressful moments. Why? Because they prepared for those very moments.

Unprepared people may buckle under that pressure: violating NCAA rules in college basketball, taking steroids in other sports, succumbing to insider trading in business. They may point fingers at others instead of accepting responsibility. That's the quickest way to kill camaraderie. It can turn a cohesive team into a jealous, backbiting group filled with individual agendas. Being able to handle disappointments and disagreements with grace is a great asset—so is accepting blame and sharing credit.

But there is a more basic way to improve, and it gets back to having passion, hunger, and drive for what you do: It's a desire to get better at every task that crosses your desk. That's more of a mindset than a practicable skill—but it takes repetitive effort to change your mindset. It takes continual monitoring to make sure you're trying to get better, as opposed to just trying to get by.

Are your interactions with employees constructive and beneficial to the company's big picture? If not, seek to improve your interpersonal skills.

Do you know everything there is to know about your marketplace and the competition? If not, more homework could be in order.

Do you have a clear vision of the direction your company is headed? If not, you might need to put a tangible plan on paper.

Most of us have parts of our job that are endured more than embraced. We should examine those areas and determine how we can do them better—thus, make them more enjoyable. The things we don't enjoy often are the things we're not good at, and avoiding those things can make a bad situation worse. That's why I try to force myself to complete the least enjoyable tasks first, every day.

The steps toward improvement generally require seeking and accepting feedback from colleagues and superiors. Most of us fight the bare truth of honest feedback, but it's critical in striving to be great. That's why we watch film of every game and every practice, for feedback on our performance and how to better it. At the end of every film session, I tell my players: The tape never lies. You may lie to yourself, but the tape tells the truth.

I remember being invited to speak to a group of salespeople at a Wall Street firm several years ago. In the words of the firm's CEO, they were all "hitting it out of the park," but their arrogance was ruining relationships within their business. They were rude, condescending, and critical of those they worked with. It was my job to get them to realize that their behavior was lowering the self-esteem of their coworkers and killing the fiber of the company. I tried the Socratic method, asking them questions designed to provoke insight and reveal the truth.

After 30 minutes of asking them questions, I could not get one of these young businesspeople to admit to a single frailty. In their minds they were never rude, critical, or condescending toward others in their firm. I was preaching to the wrong choir. This group was not interested in feedback, not interested in becoming great. They were making a great deal of money, but they were like a basketball player averaging 30 points per game on a losing team.

I kept hammering them with questions about their workplace behavior—Were they really courteous all the time? Did they really treat support staff with respect every moment?—until a few hands finally started going up. That opened the door to more honest reflection by the group as a whole. I finally got them to open their eyes and admit to errors in their ways. We pointed out the problems and worked on ways to solve them—on how to make them great players on a winning team. A group that was very fearful of objective feedback got over that obstacle to greatness.

Feedback is necessary from colleagues and superiors, but it

doesn't need to stop there. You can provide it for yourself as well by charting your own progress. Just as we chart our players in individual instructions, I chart my own attitude every day. I've done it for years. Before going to bed, I pull out my day planner and circle the date—sometimes in red, sometimes in blue, sometimes in pencil.

If I circle it in red ink, I've done my best to make it a positive day. If I circle it in blue, I have been too negative. If I circle it in pencil, the day was neutral: neither positive nor negative. My goal is to have 98 percent positive days every month. At the end of the month I total it up and see how I've done.

The best I've done for a season is to average 70 percent positive days, so there is work to do. I still have a goal to strive toward. At the end of the month, I cannot lie to myself: The numbers are there in front of me, in red and blue and gray. The numbers do not deceive—they're an honest evaluation of my improvement, day by day and week by week.

I no longer just chart my attitude. Before I go to bed every night, I write down four letters on the back of one of my omnipresent note cards: B, L, D, S. That's breakfast, lunch, dinner, and snacks. Next to each one I record everything I eat at every meal, and approximate the calories for each. Then I write down my exercise for the day. I evaluate that information to determine whether I'm adhering to my goal of staying fit and trim, and whether I need to make any adjustments the following day. If, for instance, I overdid the carbohydrates on a Tuesday, I will adjust and make Wednesday a carb-free zone.

Given the emphasis we put on physical fitness and conditioning in our program, it would be hypocritical of me to let my body go while demanding that my players push themselves into peak shape. And just like with charting my attitude, the numbers don't lie. If you don't write the stuff down, you can forget things, or you can minimize indulgences in your mind while still believing you're on task, when you're really slipping. Putting it down in writing reduces the chance of conning yourself.

It may seem a little unusual, a little anal, to play that type of game, but the one thing I've learned in 30 years of coaching is that you cannot achieve any form of greatness unless you have personal accountability on a daily basis. Set your goals high, work to achieve them, and monitor your progress without unnecessarily gilding the lily.

That's how I build my psychological report card, graded on a PHD curve. Next we'll examine how to continue earning good grades from yourself, even when distractions enter the picture.

## *Achieving Greatness*

**REBOUND RULES:**

✦ **Work hard, but do more than that.** Work deliberately, with specific drills to practice what will carry you toward a goal of greatness.

✦ **Perfect your first task before moving on to your second.** Don't dabble with Plan B until you've mastered Plan A.

✦ **Enhance your brand, pushing it from good to great.** Then maintain your process of discipline to prevent a backslide from great to good.

**POINTS OF CAUTION:**

✦ **Don't rush it.** Achieving greatness is a slow, painstaking process. Expecting it overnight is an invitation to disappointing yourself.

✦ **Don't shun feedback.** If you do, you'll keep repeating the same mistakes.

✦ **Don't rely on memory when evaluating yourself.** Write it down and face yourself with the facts.

# Chapter Seven

# Maintaining Focus

**E**VERY PERSON IN BUSINESS and sports who has attained any level of success loses focus at one point in time. It's human nature. You achieve something based on years of hard work, and your first instinct is to quit working so hard and find something more enjoyable to do. The distractions might be materialistic or socially related. When you lose focus, you tend to delegate more, take more time off, and you use the excuse that you're spending more time with your family. The truth is, you're really not spending more time with your family—you're just settling for an easier daily routine than what got you to the top to begin with.

Successful people are at risk of forgetting where they came from. They often lose touch with the young professional who worked 16-hour days to attain a loftier position. They sometimes forget about the child who dreamed of being in the spotlight as an entertainer or athlete. They occasionally find the responsibilities that come with fame and wealth to be more a burden than a privilege. Case in point: a routine ball signing when I was with the Celtics. When requests came in for signed basketballs for a charity or a school or an individual, the players would pass the balls around the locker room, sign them, and then deposit them in a bag in the center. Then I would sign them. Once, when I removed the balls from the bag, I found that only two players had legible signatures. The balls were covered with indecipherable scrawls.

I got on the guys. I said, "You work all your life to get to the point where people want your autograph, and nobody can even read your signature. Every ounce of perspiration you left on the playgrounds, every hour you put into footwork drills and conditioning and studying film—all of that was done to reach this level and play for the Boston Celtics. Don't scribble your name and number. Be proud of your name and number that you worked so hard to make valuable."

Those are the small, tedious tasks you have to take pride in. The little things you don't get credit for are part of your character, because they're not done for any reward. These little things can be the difference between winning and losing, success and failure. This is where extreme discipline and self-motivation are necessities when it comes to maintaining focus. Before you motivate others, you must motivate yourself to lead by example. Whatever task is on your plate, make it the only thing in your life at that particular time and do it to your full potential.

When we start practice, we always tell our players this: When they cross the lines onto the court, they cannot be anywhere else. It's not possible. They cannot be back in the dorm relaxing or out with their girlfriends, so while they're here, why not be the very best they can be? Practice is the task at hand; excel at it. To make that message effective, we as coaches must approach practice the same way: total focus with maximum enthusiasm. When you go through the motions, you tacitly give players the leeway to do the same. When you hit the court brimming with energy, it will spread throughout the team. When people see the tedious tasks being accomplished enthusiastically, it should produce a domino effect throughout your organization.

The people you lead must see someone committed to the cause. The danger comes when coaches and other leaders start branching out into areas beyond their expertise—areas outside of what they do best. Without question, it's very healthy in business and sports to have outside interests—meaningful distractions to any passion—but you can't lose focus on the fundamentals of what makes you successful, what you do best, and what value you have to your team.

Which brings me to Digger Phelps. When I was in college at Massachusetts in the early 1970s, he was a young coach just getting started at Fordham University. He made a lasting impression on me as a future star in the coaching business and went on to enjoy some great successes as a basketball coach—but I believe he lost focus. When I was at UMass, nobody wanted to play the Minutemen at our gym, Curry-Hicks Cage. It was quaint, small, and loud—but most of all, visiting teams had to deal with Dr. J, Julius Erving, a future Hall of Famer and one of the true greats of the game. Opponents would succumb to our home-court advantage, and the talent of the good Doctor.

But one night, an undersized, upstart Fordham team came into the Cage with an unorthodox lineup—a six-foot-six center surrounded by a bunch of guards—and upset us. The Rams pressed us all over the court. They were quicker and better at all phases of the game. They didn't have any Dr. Js on their roster, but they had five players who totally understood their style of play and bought into their coach's system.

As a young basketball player with an eye on a future coaching career, I was struck by how they played for Phelps. Years later, I studied Digger as he moved to Notre Dame and took its basketball program to new heights. Early in his tenure, the Fighting Irish ended UCLA's 88-game winning streak and spent much of the 1973–74 season ranked in the top five nationally. A few years later, he took Notre Dame to the 1978 Final Four. Digger was a charismatic leader, a cagey motivator, and a creative strategist, and he created a spirit and style that has not been matched since by the Fighting Irish. As a young coach, I was sure Digger would go on to have a long and legendary career in college basketball.

However, when I went to hear Digger speak at a coaching clinic in Cherry Hill, New Jersey, in the early 1980s, I was disappointed. Instead of talking basketball to an audience that clearly was there to hear his observations on the sport, he launched a dissertation on world affairs and politics. In one sense, he showed a well-rounded intellectual base—but on the other hand, I thought he was losing focus on being a great basketball coach. He started to stray from the building blocks of his own success.

Whether it was a coincidence or not, Digger's career at Notre Dame tailed off significantly during the 1980s and he resigned under pressure in 1991. He is a successful analyst for ESPN today, but I believed Digger's departure from the game came too early in his career. Every time I'm with Digger, I tell him he needs to get back in the game and give coaching one more shot. I see the wheels turning in his head, thinking about it, but I'm sure he's enjoying his TV gig way too much to return to the coaching grind.

I cannot say for certain that Digger lost focus, but I know this: You cannot stray from the basic building blocks of what you do. You must maintain your own discipline—for yourself and within your team or company. Even when the difficult aspects of your job become tedious and joyless, you cannot let your effort slide in those areas.

Again, this is reverting to your PHD fundamentals—the things that made you successful. The times when we're most susceptible to losing them are when things are going very well or very poorly. Both the highs and the lows can be temptations to get away from our inner game plan. There's already been discussion in this book about the challenges of sticking to what made you successful in times of crisis or personal adversity; the same steps should be followed in periods of prosperity in order to maintain focus.

In training myself to stay on task, I've started listing the three most tedious things about my job—then making them my top priorities. For me, those three things are writing letters to recruits, recruiting phone calls to people advising a prospect, and dealing with alums and e-mail. I've decided to move all those things to the forefront of my daily schedule; those will be the tasks I attack right away, when I'm full of energy. After that, everything will be smooth sailing. In basketball, recruiting is the single most important aspect of a successful program. If focus is lost in that area, failure is inevitable. But it's also the hardest work: the grueling travel; the effort to establish relationships with AAU coaches, high school coaches, and others influential in a player's life; the importance of being in constant contact with the young man and his family; the time spent stroking delicate egos.

When I took over for Denny Crum at Louisville, it was evident he still could coach and teach the game. The obvious failure was in recruiting—it lagged way behind the other facets of the program. In his late 50s and early 60s, Denny encountered a common problem: He no longer enjoyed the tedium of phone calls to coaches, letters to prospects, and traveling around the country to see them play. As other schools advanced and modernized their recruiting techniques, Louisville had a hard time keeping up. Thus my first few years, we did not have the caliber of players Crum led to two national titles and six Final Fours. Without talent around you, any coach or CEO can slip into mediocrity. With talent around you, your skills as a motivator, teacher, and leader will not erode.

That's why I respect a couple of other Hall of Famers who are still at it, Syracuse's Jim Boeheim and Connecticut's Jim Calhoun. They're both at ages where a decline in recruiting would be expected, yet they're still attracting highly ranked players every year. They have not lost track of what made them successful, and they have not abdicated all the duties they must perform to attract great talent. At the summer camps that can become so monotonous, many coaches only show up for the afternoon games. Calhoun still gets there in the morning to watch players working on fundamental drill stations—he's checking their attitude and passion for the grunt work that improves their game.

In business, the 6:45 A.M. staff meetings can be the equivalent of watching drill stations. They lose their allure. They're no longer attractive to your lifestyle, but those meetings define your work ethic and set the tone for each day in your office. Give them up at your peril.

You also should be cautious about giving away your company's identity in pursuit of growth. Home Depot remains one of the world's biggest retailers, but it gradually lost part of what got it there: a tremendous service culture. Founders Arthur Blank and Bernie Marcus made a pro-customer ethos a signature of their business, with their orange-aproned work staff building a reputation for being available, involved, and helpful. However, as Home Depot grew and became more corporate under Bob Nardelli this decade, it lost touch with the basics of great service. That difference of emphasis allowed competitor Lowe's to consume a decent-sized chunk of Home Depot's market share. In May of 2007, Home Depot's slumping stock price triggered calls at the annual shareholders convention for a change of course back to the service culture.

"I want you to know how badly we need more aprons on the floor," said Gary Patton, a 16-year Home Depot employee from South Carolina, according to Reuters. "I just long for the days back in the beginning when we were the destination store. Now we're just one of the other stores."

Home Depot's lost focus really was a change of focus as it changed coaches, from Marcus and Blank to Nardelli and to current CEO Frank Blake. Other corporations that become expansion obsessed can lose their focus along the way by diversifying without focus.

Dedicated diversification, like dedicated practice, can be a great thing. It certainly helped GE and Disney become corporate giants. But when diversification becomes unfocused, it can lead successful companies into troubled territory.

The AOL-Time Warner merger of 2000 is a classic case. Two companies with little synergy merged largely because they were huge and wanted to become even bigger. AOL purchased Time Warner for $164 billion, and two years later the megacompany reported the megaloss of $99 billion—at the time the biggest loss ever for a single company.

Also in 2000, Ford Motor Co. acquired Land Rover. Back in 1989, it had acquired Jaguar. In 2008, it sold both to a truck-making company in India for $2.3 billion—less than half of what it paid for the high-end car companies. Ford lost its focus when it made those ill-fated acquisitions.

In 1994, Quaker Oats grabbed up Snapple for $1.7 billion, a startling overpayment. It also misidentified the consumer audience for Snapple, targeting the grocery-store market for a beverage that had mostly been bought in convenience stores. Three years later, Quaker Oats unloaded Snapple for $300 million, a loss of $1.4 billion.

McDonald's has had to fight through something of an identity crisis as well, trying to reshape itself as America's eating habits have changed while simultaneously retaining its strengths. As the fast-food restaurant terrain changed, McDonald's was saddled with a reputation for low-quality food and service. Its market share eroded for a time earlier this decade before the corporation regrouped and regained its footing in recent years.

In 2001, electric component giant Tyco Electronics Corp. made the unwise decision to diversify into the financial sector by purchasing CIT Group, a leading source of financing and leasing capital, for $10 billion. A year later it made an IPO of $4.6 billion.

More recently, Citigroup began 2008 by hemorrhaging money. It posted a $10 billion loss in the fourth quarter of 2007 in part due to what *U.S. News & World Report* termed "its headlong dive into complex financial instruments tied to borrowers with shaky credit histories." That led to an announcement that thousands of jobs would be cut worldwide.

Simply put, you can't lose sight of who you are, what you do best, what you're trying to accomplish, and what your goals are. That includes an unwavering commitment to tackle the tedious tasks and unpleasant challenges as soon as they present themselves. The more you succeed, the harder it can be to stay on task—not just as a commercial entity, but as an individual. It's when the weekly round of golf becomes twice a week or more. It's the excuse that you're entertaining clients, so you're on the golf course or on your speedboat, or out on the town. It's when you're suddenly busy doing everything but what you do best. You've lost focus on the job at hand.

If you want to maintain the lifestyle you've built and come to enjoy, you can't lose focus—until it's time for you to pass the baton to someone else.

Now, that doesn't mean I'm an advocate of sleeping on the couch in your office for weeks at a time. There are too many coaches—and undoubtedly too many CEOs—who have turned their jobs into obsessions that eliminate family, friends, and fun from their lives. Outside interests can keep you stimulated in other areas and keep you from burning out your passion. I have a lot of diversity in my life, both financially and in terms of hobbies, but I strive to keep it in balance.

Occasionally I play golf—I'm not very good at it, but for me it's a welcome stress reliever. I'm an avid investor and have a number of different business interests, but I've hired a trusted adviser to monitor my investments and I check in with him monthly. I'm into the thoroughbred business, but I don't micromanage the men who train my horses, and my time at the track is limited to three days at Del Mar in August, a week at Saratoga, and a couple of days at Churchill Downs for the Kentucky Oaks and Kentucky Derby. Everything else is watching on television. For that two-week period at the track, it's a great distraction, but it doesn't take a lot of energy to watch your horses—it's not like training for a marathon. It's a means of relaxation, a chance to decompress, and it doesn't infringe on the crucial aspects of my job.

Finding a way to relieve stress is more important than finding a way to escape pressure. I've always said you want pressure; you don't want stress. Pressure is what every competitor looks for: in pharmaceutical sales, in life insurance, in automobile sales. It's what makes a $2 game of golf mean as much as a $100 game—you're competing to win and putting the pressure on yourself to do your best—but you've got to be able to walk a tightrope between meaningful distraction and a loss of motivation. Meticulous focus must be maintained to achieve greatness in your chosen endeavor. Once you lose focus, your foundation cracks and your competition will overcome you.

Failure can undercut a career, if you don't deal with it productively, or complacency can set in after a great achievement. It can be surprisingly easy to drift.

In May 2008, tennis player Justine Henin became the first woman player ever to retire while ranked No. 1 in the world. She had reached the ripe old age of 25. Henin said she no longer needed tennis to feel happy. Hopefully that remains true for her.

Golfer David Duval is a famous case—he started having injuries, then swing problems, and then his focus seemed to wane. One day, he was the No. 1 golfer in the world and Tiger Woods' potential rival for years to come, and the next he was more interested in snowboarding.

"Even before his golf ball started going sideways, Duval had been suffering from a deteriorating competitive soul," wrote John Hawkins of *GolfWorld* in 2007. "His desire to play the game at its highest level, even for millions of dollars and on his own terms, had dwindled to the point where the negatives outweighed the positives."

As one of the top money-winners of all time, Duval could monetarily survive his loss of professional focus. That's one of the great culprits—if you're only in it for the paycheck, and not for the passion, it's easy to become sidetracked. A while back, Duval started a comeback, and it transformed his public persona from an aloof, disliked golfer to a sympathetic figure. Perhaps he realized that he needed stimulus, needed a challenge, needed something more than money could buy him.

Greg Norman is another golfer who seemingly lost interest and lost focus, perhaps partly due to a succession of agonizing losses in major tournaments. Norman steadily became more absorbed in designing courses and in the golf equipment business, luxury boats, sport fishing, and even wine making. There is nothing wrong with any of that, but his pursuit of greatness was compromised along the way. (Let's hope his runner-up finish at the British Open, at age 53, is a sign of late-career passion.)

For those who lose focus, there are fewer safety nets in business than in sports. In the NBA, players in the last year of their contract become more motivated to play well and sign that next contract. In business, people don't have 6–8–10-year contracts for $10 million a year like they do in sports. You have to maintain that focus every day.

The athletes who can do that are among the most unique on the planet. Tiger Woods. Jerry Rice. Peyton Manning. Michael Jordan. For all their fame and glory, they never lost sight of what made them great and never stopped working to improve—yet even they could have bad days. They are human. Not everybody's going to be on top of their game every day. That needs to be understood by any boss—a margin of human error must be factored in. For a million different reasons, office productivity can be compromised by having a bad day—but if you stay locked in on your goals and what you hope to achieve, you'll bring out your best most of the time. Your goal is to achieve maximum performance on a daily basis, and to help those around you do the same. Set that goal and then try like hell to attain it.

John Wooden was the best at it, because he maintained a level of excellence built on excellent daily habits and routines. He retired at the relatively young age of 64, probably because he didn't think he could maintain it any longer. But for a long period of time, he was as disciplined and focused a basketball coach as we've ever had in this game.

Wooden is a man of great humility and modest means—when he coached, he never worried about leading a luxurious lifestyle or playing three rounds of golf a week. He was very focused on doing what he had to do to be a great motivator, communicator, and teacher. Even in retirement, the same principles guide his daily life. He was a child of an austere upbringing in a simpler time, in Martinsville, Indiana, and that has never left him.

Wooden is a good example of the fact that in every instance where you're trying to outwork your competitor, there has to be a common denominator. A better life for me isn't good enough. It has to be a better life for my family and for people around me. You cannot waste time obsessing over the court of public opinion.

When it comes to maintaining focus amid excessive criticism or excessive praise, one saying can help: What other people have to say about me is none of my business. That doesn't mean you should tune out thoughtful feedback, but you have to filter out the stuff that will superficially inflate or damage your self-esteem.

A great example of this was my days coaching the New York Knicks during the 1988–89 season. We lived outside Manhattan, and I had a driver named Walter who took me to Madison Square Garden on game days. One day, after a grueling five-game road trip, Walter asked me if I wanted to listen to some music. I said no, I'd rather just shut my eyes for a while. Then he asked me if I wanted to listen to the hottest thing on the radio: WFAN, all-sports talk radio.

Sure, I said, figuring that it would be nice to hear a few compliments on the way to the Garden. We were playing really well at the time, in the middle of a club-record 26-game home winning streak and on our way to winning the Atlantic Division for the first time since 1970–71. But compliments were not in the airwaves when Walter turned on WFAN. The first caller was Vinny from Bensonhurst, and he said I should be fired tomorrow. He said we were pressing too much and would have no legs left by the playoffs.

At that point, I nearly jumped into the front seat with Walter.

The second caller was Mike from Bay Ridge. He said, "I couldn't agree any more with Vinny. Pitino should be fired immediately. They shoot too many threes and don't play any half-court basketball." I was shocked. I asked Walter, "Does this go on all the time?" His response to this day makes me laugh. "No, coach. They love you. You should hear what they say about the Jet and Giant coaches. And their families."

I figured out that listening to sports talk radio was not going to build my self-esteem. I immediately reverted back to my Eagles and Creedence Clearwater Revival tapes.

My boss during my previous stint with the Knicks, Hubie Brown, wasn't as successful at tuning out the critics. Hubie taught me more about basketball in two years as his assistant coach than I could have learned from anyone else in 10—but he was easily distracted by the criticism of the New York media.

He thought certain writers from the tabloids were out to get him. I knew some of those writers, and during those times (the mid-1980s) you could have a beer or go out to dinner with them on road trips. I knew for a fact that they liked and respected Hubie—but they were in competition for readers and tried to be controversial to sell newspapers. So they took some shots at him.

I tried to get Hubie to ignore their articles completely, or to simply understand the nature of the New York media beast. His response was, "They're not talking about you." He was correct, of course, but you can't lose focus because of meaningless criticism from the outside. It just clutters up your mind.

Situations like those are why I view the mind as a cluttered desk. It needs to be cleaned up; get the useless stuff out of there. Don't complicate your thought processes with insignificant things. Did it really matter what Vinny from Bensonhurst was saying about whether the Knicks pressed too much? Did it really matter whether a reporter knocked Hubie Brown once in the course of writing nine other positive articles?

Of course not. Get rid of that mental clutter.

That's an especially hard lesson for young people to learn. They crave the superficial affirmation of others. They want virtual strangers to sign on as friends on their Facebook or MySpace pages. They seek popularity and pats on the back, often from the wrong sources—and when the feedback isn't glowing? They lose perspective.

"So-and-so is hating on you." Our players at Louisville get that all the time—in text messages, e-mails, phone calls. They get it from friends and family members and others outside our program. They sound the alarm when a magazine or website doesn't rate them among the top 10 players at their position, or doesn't rate our team in the top five. If Jay Bilas doesn't pick us to win on ESPN, it's an outrage. If Lee Corso puts something on his head to say he's picking the other team, it's a call to arms. If our players are locked in on that kind of thing, they're suffering from cluttered minds. They should be locked in on the hours of preparation that got us ready to play the game, not whether someone in the media picks us to win or lose.

That kind of stuff is hollow motivation, especially the stuff that passes as pregame bulletin board material.

Kevin Willard is one of the best assistant coaches I've ever had, but he made a silly mistake one year before we played Marquette. He made up some quotes from the head coach of Marquette dissing our guys and put it in the scouting report, thinking it would fire up our team. He did this with other teams and coaches as well.

After the Marquette game, one of our scouting reports was left in the locker room and delivered to the Golden Eagles' coaching staff. They made it public and it was a minor embarrassment. I told Kevin, "Do you really think our guys are going to rebound better or execute better because of that? It doesn't work." It may get you jumping higher in warm-ups, but that's about it. If you have to rely on contrived disrespect to get ready to play, consistency is not part of your makeup.

But it's amazing how many people enthusiastically spread what they consider bad news or disrespect. We have too many people with rabbit ears for that kind of stuff. Exhibit A is Derrick Caracter, a sophomore on our 2007–08 team, and possibly the most challenging player I have ever coached. He first gained attention as an eighth grader, growing well ahead of his classmates to reach six feet eight and 270 pounds. Derrick had stunning talent to go along with his size, and his precocious ability got him invited to several elite national camps at an early age. That made him a national curiosity, and unfortunately the attention went straight to his head.

During a high school career dotted by transfers to different schools and disciplinary suspensions for his lax work ethic, the only thing that grew for Derrick was his waistline. He was 300 pounds coming out of high school in New Jersey. Despite his troubles, we took a chance on him because of his immense talent and a seeming willingness to change his ways.

Derrick lost weight and got into shape in his first few months at Louisville, but his attitude and maturation never progressed to the point where he could be counted on every day. He was a classic microwave culture kid; spoiled by instant gratification at a young age and not willing to work toward the long haul. Derrick is not a bad guy, but he doesn't understand criticism.

One day he came into my office and said, "Everyone's knocking me." He said he was not ranked among the best players at his position by various media outlets and was not on anybody's draft lists. I told him he should be focused on improving his game and not on what other people were saying about his game. I read him a Wooden quote: "Be more concerned with your character than your reputation, because your character is what you really are, while your reputation is merely what others think you are." That and many other lessons have been hard for Derrick to grasp.

Whether you're an immature college kid or a CEO late in life, you can lose focus on what's important. That's why it's vital to check in with yourself while pursuing greatness. Are you staying on task? Are you enjoying the fruits of your success too much? Are you majoring in minors and sweating too much small stuff? All those things will distract you from reaching your goals.

Maintaining rigorous focus will keep you headed toward those goals. Sometimes, though, that focus has to be flexible enough to change and adapt to new conditions and challenges.

## *Maintaining Focus*

**REBOUND RULES:**

✦ **Stick to your strengths.** A successful businessperson isn't necessarily cut out to be a good politician or vice versa.

✦ **Stay organized.** Plan out your day, every day, and write everything down. That way nothing slips your mind.

✦ **Don't get caught up in what others are saying about you.** Repeat John Wooden's advice: "Be more concerned with your character than your reputation, because your character is what you really are, while your reputation is merely what others think you are."

**POINTS OF CAUTION:**

✦ **Don't lose sight of who you are,** what made you successful, how you accomplished it, and what your goals are.

✦ **Make sure your daily discipline remains intact,** even though true passion can make a vocation seem like a vacation.

✦ **Don't subscribe to hollow motivation.** Stay in touch with what's really driving you to succeed.

# Chapter Eight

# Creating New Ways and Improving Old Ones

**T**HERE'S BEEN A DEBATE in college basketball for the past several years about whether the three-point field goal line should be extended from its current distance of 19 feet, nine inches. The line for international basketball is 20 feet, six inches. Beginning in 2008, the college line will jump to 20 feet, nine inches. Those opposed act like the increase is a mile long. To the surprise of some people, I'm all in favor of making the change. They think that because the 19-foot-nine line has been so beneficial to my teams over its 21 years of use that I'd be resistant to tinkering with it.

I don't mind making the three-pointer longer for several reasons: One, it would open up the inside game; two, I believe we'd adapt better than most of our competitors; and three, it falls in line with one of my credos I try to live and work by: If it's not broken, break it and make it better.

On the face of it, that credo might seem at odds with the theme of the previous chapter on maintaining focus. In it, I cited examples of companies and people who altered what they did best and paid a price for it. However, I'm not talking about abandoning your bread and butter; I'm talking about refining it, modernizing it, and making it even more effective. The things that should not deviate are your work ethic and focus, the fundamental rebound rules, but your strategies and approaches should be flexible enough to change with the times.

Doing things the same way over and over can work for a while. It sets a winning foundation for your team or company—but don't wait for it to stop working before changing it up. You should always have an eye open for how to improve yourself, your team, and your business.

Why? Because your competition isn't standing still. It might be stealing ideas from you and catching up to you. That's the nature of competition—imitation is the highest form of flattery, and your opponents will imitate what you do well while simultaneously working to stop it. When Indiana's basketball team went 32–0 and won the national title in 1976 under Bob Knight, there were high schools and colleges nationwide mimicking the Hoosiers' great passing game. Meanwhile, the rest of the Big Ten conference was figuring out defenses that would slow them down. Once someone sets a standard for excellence, everyone else will attempt to both copy it and combat it.

When I returned to college coaching at Louisville after the Celtics, it was evident that teams had become better at handling full-court pressure defense and better at defending the three-point line. We couldn't continue to attack teams in 2002 the same way we did in 1997, and we couldn't rely on getting open three-pointers the same way we did in 1987. We had to break our mold and make it better.

It's no different with great companies. The 1990s cyberturf battle for control of the Internet browser market between Netscape and Microsoft was a textbook case of an industry leader being targeted and taken down by its competition. In 1997, Netscape Navigator had roughly 72 percent of the browser market, while Microsoft's Internet Explorer had 18 percent. When Microsoft held its launch party for Internet Explorer 4.0 that year in San Francisco, some cheeky employees planted the Explorer logo in the Netscape office front lawn. Netscape responded by knocking over the lowercase e and putting its own dinosaur logo atop it.

But the stunt turned out to be symbolic of a sea change. When Microsoft backed Internet Explorer with its enormous war chest—it was bundled free of charge with Windows, which had about 90 percent of the operating system market—the tide turned. Microsoft went for the jugular, and Netscape contributed to its own demise with some questionable business decisions. By 2002, Internet Explorer owned about 96 percent of the browser market. Netscape had been outflanked and beaten down by its relentless competition.

But competition can come full circle. Since 2004, Internet Explorer has seen its market share gradually eaten into by Firefox—from 92 percent in October 2004 to 75 percent in April 2008. Firefox's share has risen by a comparable margin, from 3 percent to 18 percent. Whoever is the industry leader will be targeted.

That's why all successful companies can expect the struggle to stay on top to be every bit as difficult as the struggle to arrive on top in the first place. Your areas of excellence will be put under a microscope; patents, marketing strategies, or new products will be mimicked. Your weaknesses will be picked apart and exploited. A true competitor has to stay ahead of the curve. You keep your fundamentals intact, but strive to make your business better every day.

We've all read novels or seen movies about people who hire spies to infiltrate a company to steal their ideas and their plans for new products. Although that kind of drama is mostly the stuff of fiction authors and Hollywood screenwriters, the competition everyone faces in business is real and unrelenting.

Another great business example is how Coca-Cola made a big move in 2007 to catch up to Pepsi in the race to sell noncarbonated beverages. Pepsi had taken the lead in that area, buying Quaker Oats (which makes Gatorade) and corralling 50 percent of that market to just 23 percent for Coke, according to *Beverage Digest*. So Coke made a huge corrective move by purchasing Glaceau, maker of Vitaminwater, for $4.1 billion. At the time, Coke still was the strong leader in the soda market, with 43 percent to Pepsi's 31 percent, according to the *New York Times*, but Coke foresaw a future market tilting more toward noncarbonated drinks—so it broke its highly successful model and made it better.

Nintendo did something similar with the advent of its Wii gaming console. Nintendo had gone from kingpin to a bit stale, losing ground to Sony, Microsoft, and Nokia in the competitive video-game market. It boldly broke its old model and made it better with the wireless handheld Wii, which was ranked No. 4 on a list of the most innovative products of 2006 by *PC World*. By 2007, Wii was *the* hot American Christmas gift, and everyone from kindergarteners to retirees were whacking virtual tennis balls, rolling virtual bowling balls, or punching virtual boxing opponents.

You have to understand the nature of competition. As a business leader, you shouldn't be afraid to tweak something in search of improvement. I try to do that as a coach. I put everything we do all year on tape—all the plays, all the defenses—and then I study them in April. I go through the process for three reasons: to understand what made us successful; to break it apart statistically and physically; and to try to analyze it through our competitors' eyes to make it better.

I study the defense: how we defend inside, how we play the perimeter, how we press—and how we can make each area better. Do we need more pressure on ball handlers? Should we try to deny passes to the interior? Should we trap opposing big men and create our rotations that way? Using full-court pressure at Providence induced mistakes and fatigue—but our competitors started figuring us out. We charted their success rate at finding holes in the defense and scoring uncontested baskets, and we learned where we were vulnerable. We altered our pressure to trap in speed situations, when players tried to go too fast and break the press by themselves.

Then I study our offense. I break down our shooting percentages—how many challenged shots did we take? How many open shots? How many plays worked, and why, and against whom, and when?

In general, your company can never be too in touch with both its strengths and weaknesses. Retreats and periodic managerial meetings should include time for rigorous and honest evaluation of where you stand: the good and the bad. Feedback on how to improve and innovate should always be encouraged and accepted from the rank-and-file employees. You should know your company well enough that if a stranger walks in and asks you to explain what you do well and what you can do better, the answer shouldn't include much hemming and hawing. The answers should be on the tip of your tongue.

Utilizing the most recent data available, company leaders should be able to come up with a list of the three things it does best. It also should be able to list three areas in needs to improve. Based upon our 2007–08 statistics, I made the following lists:

What we did well:

1. We forced teams to play fast and take quick shots, which resulted in us ranking eighth in the country in field-goal percentage defense.

2. We had a high number of assists (15.1 per game) despite not ranking in the top 100 in scoring, which tells me we passed the ball well.

3. We executed backdoor plays when opposing defenses pressured us.

What we need to improve:

1. Foul shooting. We ranked 293rd nationally, which is just unacceptable and very unusual for one of my teams.

2. We were not great one-on-one defenders. We improved in that area over the previous season, but still were beaten too much. That's why we had to rely on zone defense more than I generally prefer.

3. We didn't offensive rebound well enough.

How do we improve on those things? We'll make it a daily point of emphasis, for one thing. We'll incorporate drills to work on them. We'll study the teams that do those things well to see if they have any techniques we can steal. We then set goals to make everything statistically better. We base those goals on last year's data, selecting the areas where we can improve and must improve.

Businesses also should be able to produce similar lists—for themselves and regarding their prime competition. In addition, each list should generate a subset. For the list of what your company does best, you should be able to identify the most likely ways your competition will try to counteract your advantage. A different marketing campaign? A new product line? For the list of what the competition does well, you should be able to find concepts worth borrowing and implementing by your company.

Then examine your list of weaknesses. How can the competition hurt you because of them? What specific means can improve them? Are there books on the subject? Scholarly articles? Would it help to bring in an outside expert to observe your operation and mentor your workers in those areas? Can goals be set for gradual improvement? When it comes to your competition's weaknesses, your company should be able to enumerate methods for taking advantage of any openings provided.

Hopefully, your company will be filled with passionate employees who keep up on industry trends and innovations on their own, but don't take that for granted. Someone within your organization should be in charge of a clip file—preferably digital—on anything happening within your field. Ideally, that file would be updated and disseminated daily. A proactive CEO will keep his own good-ideas file, with the plan of implementing them on a monthly, quarterly, or annual basis. Make implementation a goal and then hold your firm accountable on the results: Are you keeping up with the pace of change?

We had success early in my coaching career with relentless pressure defense and three-pointers by the boatload. However, if I'd stayed with those strategies at the expense of evolving, my career might be over by now. We still press more than most and still shoot more threes than most, but that's not all we do. My recent Louisville teams have played more half-court zone defense and become more balanced offensively, because that's given us the best chance to win.

My former assistant and player Billy Donovan called me following the 2006 season, when he won his first national championship at Florida. Virtually his entire team was coming back, and he wanted to know what it would take to win back-to-back championships—something that had only been done once since John Wooden retired at UCLA in 1975. Billy also talked to Bill Belichick, Pat Riley, and Mike Krzyzewski—people who won back-to-back championships: Belichick did it with the New England Patriots, Riley with the Los Angeles Lakers, and Krzyzewski at Duke. He picked their brains on what those repeat seasons were like.

He asked me what we did in 1996–97, after winning the national title the previous year. We wound up losing our bid for a repeat in overtime in the championship game to Arizona—and if our best player, Derek Anderson, hadn't suffered a season-ending knee injury in January, I am sure we would have had a great opportunity to win it again.

I told Billy that if I were in his shoes, with the same team coming back, I'd do the same things as last year motivationally—but I'd take all the statistical things he stressed and try to do a better job. If his field-goal defense was 41 percent, I'd set a goal of getting it under 40. If the three-point defense was 32 percent, I'd try to get it under 30. If the team averaged 18 assists per game, I'd try to get it to 20. All the relevant things that make his system go, I'd try to make them two points better statistically.

That's what I tried to do in 1997. If we were getting 35 deflections per game, we tried to get it closer to 40. We would try to overcome the loss of overwhelming talent with an increase in hustle—and deflections are the clearest way to gauge that vague dynamic. If your players are active—in the face of the man they're guarding, waving their hands, sprinting back to help on defense—they're going to get their hands on the ball. When you demand great effort from your players, that's the one place it will show up statistically. That's why we assign an assistant coach to do nothing but chart deflections, by player, for every game. Certain statistics don't lie, and they pan out over a period of time.

I don't know how much all the feedback Billy got wound up helping his repeat quest, but the Gators got it done. They had a second successive dominant NCAA tournament run to win the '07 title and earn a place among the great teams in recent college basketball history. I was so impressed with the fact that Billy was striving to improve his system, and went to great lengths to seek out people to help him break it and make it better.

Part of any sustained greatness is staying hungry, even after reaching the mountaintop. However, it also requires a willingness to keep learning and a refusal to fall back on the same old habits.

There are many examples of the power of proactive thinking in the business world. Toyota became an international automotive leader through the 1980s and 1990s, but it stayed miles ahead of the curve with its innovative development of hybrid vehicles. The company started work on an environmentally friendly vehicle in 1994, and had the Prius on the Japanese market in 1997 and the European market in 2001. Prius was Motor Trend Car of the Year in 2004 and has outsold all other hybrid vehicles combined. That sort of thing doesn't happen by accident. In fact, it's literally written into the corporate culture. One of the five Toyota precepts is a commitment to "be at the vanguard of the times through endless creativity, inquisitiveness and pursuit of improvement."

At GE, Jack Welch broke the mold and made it better. He deconstructed a massive bureaucracy and remade it, streamlining a huge company and changing its identity. What once was solely an industrial giant that made things became a global service provider, with assets in the hundreds of billions to show for the change. No wonder *Fortune* named Welch "Manager of the Century" in 1999.

Apple's Steve Jobs has continually found ways to modernize his company and stay ahead of his competition. As *BusinessWeek* put it a few years ago: "More than anyone else, he brought digital technology to the masses. As a visionary, he saw that computers could be much more than drab productivity tools. Instead, they could help unleash human creativity and sheer enjoyment. A marketing genius, he conceived of elegant products that captured consumers' imaginations. And as a relentless perfectionist, he came up with creations that actually delivered on their promise— raising the bar for rivals."

Similarly, the British rock band Radiohead raised the bar for rivals and record labels alike, with its daring decision to make its album, *In Rainbows*, available online to listeners at whatever price they deemed appropriate. That was certainly a new twist on the old way of selling music. In doing so, Radiohead might have dealt a lethal blow to the traditional record-label business, while broadening the means by which music consumers interact with the musicians they enjoy.

Entire cities have found ways to reinvent themselves and improve their outlooks. Pittsburgh, once dependent upon a declining steel industry, now is a vibrant technology and health care city.

On the flip side, there also are plenty of cautionary tales of being caught flat-footed while those around you are making upgrades and changes. Levi Strauss & Co. lost a hammerlock on the American jean market, recording declining sales nine out of 10 years from 1997–2006. The newspaper industry, slow to capitalize on the explosive growth of the Internet and to take on the challenge of TV, has been cannibalizing itself this century in an attempt to stave off obsolescence.

The fact is most fresh knowledge comes from without, not from within. Everyone is constantly on the lookout for fresh ideas, including ones that come from nontraditional sources. That might be why one *Wall Street Journal* list of the most influential business thinkers included some unexpected names. Among them were *New York Times* columnist Thomas Friedman, *Blink* author Malcolm Gladwell, and Harvard professor Howard Gardner. They bring different ideas to the table— thoughts on how the world is changing (Friedman) and how the mind works (Gardner)—that can be applied to business theories and practices.

Like business leaders, I try to absorb everything that I can get my hands on that will help me in my profession. I try to read, dissect, and integrate on a daily basis. For instance, my wife is always asking me why I watch so much NBA basketball. The answer: I'm always looking for a great sideline out-of-bounds play to steal. In the NBA, they run great last-second plays and they're great strategists in timeouts. I'm spending 2½ hours watching a game just to find a few seconds that could help our team.

When I see that one moment that makes the studying worthwhile, I'm ready to commit it to paper with my trusty note cards. I keep them next to me whenever I'm watching a basketball game on TV. On the back of them, I have half-court diagrams. In just an instant, I can jot down the play I saw on my prepared diagram and have it to show to my staff the next morning. Once again, I don't want to rely on memory; I want to get it right. That means getting it down, in writing, right away.

Almost every interaction is a chance to learn something, an educational opportunity. If I wind up sitting next to you on a plane, I'm going to ask you two questions: What is the best vacation you've ever taken, and have you read any great motivational books? The first question is for my family. We're always searching for a new getaway destination. (Last summer, it was a whitewater rafting trip.) The second question is for my profession—because I'm constantly on the lookout for fresh motivational angles and ideas.

You can find useful nuggets of information almost anywhere if you're looking for them. I'm a voracious reader, so I'll constantly be scanning newspapers and magazines for articles that can apply to coaching. Current events can sometimes affect how we do our business as well—for instance, the economy can influence recruiting. The skyrocketing costs of transportation can be a deterrent to crisscrossing the country to see recruits and be seen by them. If private planes are no longer a cost-effective means of travel, what will take their place? Perhaps it's video conferencing. Alabama football coach Nick Saban already has done some of that in recruiting, and you can be sure it will be copied if it meets a need.

I'm also interested in the latest trends in conditioning and nutrition. If I'm on the treadmill, I might flip on five minutes of *Oprah*, just in case she has a particularly inspirational guest. I'm in search of anything that might help me get better as a coach; anything I can integrate into tomorrow's plan for improving myself and my program.

If the opportunity presents itself, I will even pick the brains of my competitors for information on our team. There have been times when I've run into opposing coaches on airplanes, in hotels, or in a gym and asked them for a quick scouting report on us. What did you see that you could exploit? What did you think we did well? When Tom Crean was the coach at Marquette, we went at it with maximum ferocity—it was a great rivalry based on respect, but when we were on the same sidelines, it was a contentious battle. I saw Tom at the 2008 Final Four, after he'd just left Marquette to take the Indiana job, and we had a frank and productive discussion about what we saw in each other's teams. I knew Tom's assessment of our team would be valuable because he's such a thorough scouter, and hopefully the feedback I gave him was equally useful.

College basketball coaches are extremely competitive, but also collegial enough that we'll usually give candid answers to another coach searching for ways to improve his team. Just be willing to give information, as well as receive, however; the feedback for both parties can be very valuable.

When I do find something new I want to integrate with my team, it has to be adapted to the particular strengths and weaknesses of our personnel. My Louisville team cannot run a carbon copy of the Phoenix Suns offense without Steve Nash at point guard, and neither can a small corporation adopt the Microsoft business plan lock, stock, and barrel. But everyone borrows concepts, so why not borrow from the best?

In fact, there are very few completely original concepts out there, in sports or in business. Oftentimes, the biggest winners are the best adapters—those who can take someone else's good idea, tweak it, and fit it to the best available talent. Urban Meyer and Rich Rodriguez both got in near the ground floor on the spread offense as college football assistant coaches, but as head coaches, they have built their versions of it in different ways—both with great success. Meyer's teams have thrown the ball more on the way to breakthrough seasons at Utah and Florida—he took the Utes to an undefeated season in 2004, and the Gators to the national championship in 2006. Meanwhile, Rodriguez utilized a more run-based version of the spread in leading West Virginia to three Big East championships in the last four years. Now he's moved on to Michigan, where he's modified it further to suit the players he has inherited.

The main motivation for creating new ways to do business and improving upon old ones is to keep your work fresh and accelerate your company's growth—to keep learning and avoid standing still. You never know when or where some stray bit of wisdom will appear. You definitely won't find it if you don't seek it.

I opened this chapter talking about the three-point shot, and I'll close it by talking about how it created a new way to succeed in college basketball. In 1986–87, my Providence team was the innovative competitor that caught everyone else standing pat, thanks to the three. That rule change helped take us on a fairy-tale ride to the Final Four—because we embraced it.

Going into the season, I knew we didn't have Top 50 talent—and I was very concerned about our ability to compete in a Big East conference that was formidable. Not only was there great talent, but there also were Hall of Fame coaches like Rollie Massimino of Villanova, Louie Carnesecca of St. John's, and John Thompson of Georgetown.

I studied all three of them, their stats, and their personnel. I figured if they had one weakness we could exploit, it was that they wouldn't significantly change with the new three-point rule. Their background of success dictated that they'd keep doing what they'd been doing. They would live by the opposite of my credo: If it's not broken, why fix it?

Because our program wasn't as far along, I had no problem daring to break it and making it better. The basic math formula said you only had to shoot 33 percent from three-point range to get the same benefits as shooting 50 percent from two-point range, and we had some guys who could really stroke it. So I set up three goals for that year regarding the three-point shot: We wanted to lead the country in three-pointers made; we would try to gain a significant advantage from the three-point line by limiting our opponents' threes with our perimeter defense; and we would incorporate the three into all our special situations. We'd look for the shot on baseline inbounds plays, sideline inbounds, in transition, after offensive rebounds, and off pick-and-roll plays late in the shot clock.

Coming into that season, I hoped we'd shoot 15 or 16 threes per game and make five or six. But after playing an exhibition game against a Russian team, I realized those numbers were way too low. We made six of 16 threes while the Russians made nine of 28—a nine-point advantage for them. At that time the foreign teams were more advanced in their use of the three-point shot. I broke down that tape for hours and learned a lot about utilizing the three-point shot. It spurred me to increase our goals to 20–25 threes attempted per game and eight–10 made. There in the latter stages of the Cold War, the Russians finally found a way to help us.

The result of this strategic shift was startling. We were way ahead of the curve. In our first five Big East games that season, our opponents attempted a total of fewer than 10 three-point shots and didn't make any. In two games, they didn't even attempt a three.

Did that mean Rollie, Louie, and Big John were too stubborn to change? Absolutely not. It just meant that it wasn't an easy transition from hunting layups to hunting 20-foot jump shots. They didn't believe in doing anything with an offensive rebound other than powering it back up to the basket. And running set plays to produce long jumpers? That would have been heresy.

Meanwhile, my heretics at Providence wound up leading the nation that year in threes per game at 8.24. Our success that season sent me to my next job, as coach of the New York Knicks, and then on to championship success at Kentucky. At both of those stops, we were well ahead of the competition when it came to capitalizing on the three. We've kind of grown up together, the three and me. Looking back at the arc of my career, I'm not sure where I'd be if we didn't create new ways and improve old ones.

## *Creating New Ways and Improving Old Ones*

**REBOUND RULES:**

✦ **If it's not broken, break it and make it better.** Don't be afraid to tinker with your game plan.

✦ **Understand your competition.** Scout them and know their strengths and weaknesses as well as you know your own.

✦ **Use statistical data to chart improvements,** in big and small steps.

**POINTS OF CAUTION:**

✦ **Don't stagnate.** "We've always done it that way" is not a good reason for continuing to do it that way. See if there's a better way.

✦ **Don't stifle creative ideas.** Encourage a free-flowing climate of innovative thought.

✦ **Don't shut down your communication base after experiencing success.** You can still learn from others outside your sphere, if you'll listen to them.

## Chapter Nine
# *Surround Yourself with Future Leaders*

**I** **TELL EVERY ASSISTANT** coaching candidate I interview, "I don't hire assistants. I hire future head coaches." For proof of this, look at the team picture from our first year at Kentucky. One day it might be worth shipping to the college basketball Hall of Fame. My staff of Ralph Willard, Herb Sendek, Tubby Smith, and Billy Donovan all went on to become head coaches, with tremendous results: three national championships (two for Donovan and one for Smith); at least one NCAA tournament Sweet Sixteen appearance for each coach; and a total of 1,328 collegiate victories heading into the 2008–09 season.

But that's just one staff. I've been incredibly fortunate to hire or recruit future top coaches at every stop in my career. More than 20 of my former assistants or players have gone on to become college head coaches, and a couple of them have become head coaches in the NBA.

One of the most rewarding parts of my job is seeing the people I have tutored move on to have success of their own in our chosen profession. When Billy Donovan won that first national title at Florida in 2006, I had a better feeling inside than when we won it at Kentucky 10 years earlier. The pride I felt was immense.

That night, I was nervously sitting with Joanne and Billy's wife, Christine, a few rows up across from the Florida bench in Indianapolis' RCA Dome. The nerves were short-lived, as the Gators dominated the entire game. Shortly after the final buzzer, after embracing his assistants and players and shaking hands with the vanquished Bruins, Billy was looking up toward us, gesturing. "He wants you to go down there, Christine," I told her—but security came up and escorted me to the floor.

When I got there, I wrapped my arms around Billy and told him that this should be his stage, not mine. Billy said, "I wouldn't be here enjoying this moment if it hadn't been for you. I love you." At that point I couldn't let go of him, because I didn't want the crowd of photographers around us to see that I had tears in my eyes.

As a result of Billy's success at Florida, he has had several assistants of his own go on to Division I head coaching jobs: John Pelphrey (who played for me at Kentucky) is the head coach at Arkansas; Anthony Grant is the head coach at Virginia Commonwealth; and Donnie Jones is the head coach at Marshall. I see Billy handing down some of the same lessons I did to him, continuing a legacy. It's a great thing.

"The big thing was the level of responsibility given to us," Billy said of his time at Kentucky as my assistant. "We were taught how to make decisions. But to make those decisions, we had to be thorough and on top of what was going on. And if we made a mistake, it had better not be from a lack of work. I've tried to carry that over in working with my own assistants," Billy continued. "I want to throw all of them into situations where they'll have a chance to learn enough to be ready to be head coaches when the time comes. They should understand all areas of the job: coaching, teaching, recruiting, organization, dealing with the media. A lot of other guys don't get that chance."

However, you have to hire the right people to begin with— people cut out to one day lead a basketball team or a company. You're not necessarily looking for friends or loyal companions. Those factors can be significant, but the main goal is to enhance your organization with talented, hard-working people who will move on and build your success tree.

That's a key point: Don't be afraid to hire assistants who will leave you. If you're hiring people nobody else wants, how much good are they doing for your company? You have to be willing to risk turnover if it means you're bringing in quality workers. It actually will help your talent recruitment.

If you establish a track record of hiring bright, energetic employees who go on to future success, it will only enhance your reputation among motivated young professionals. When you lose one, you'll have a slew of qualified applicants to replace him or her—because they'll see you as a CEO who nurtures their career goals. They'll see your company as a pipeline to success. Furthermore, when you do lose one, you'll have others on hand to help you continue your winning streak.

Toward that end, I always sit down and imagine the coaches I'm interviewing running their own program—eventually. I don't want to hire guys who spend two years doing nothing but trying to network for a head-coaching job. As we discussed earlier, I want assistants who know their role and will perform it without worrying about getting public credit for it. When they've done that, I'll go to bat for them in the job market—usually with good results. But during that first interview, I want to be able to see something that tells me they'll eventually be successful leaders of a team, or I look elsewhere. I need to see some leadership capability along with the passion, hunger, and drive.

It's also important to have a diverse staff that will allow all parties to be constantly stimulated. If everyone in your meetings looks alike, talks alike, and thinks alike, your pool of ideas is probably pretty shallow and stale. I like it when my assistants bring a new wrinkle or strategy thought to our early-morning staff meetings, so we can discuss the merits of it and how we might implement it. Creative thinking should be fostered, and everyone on your staff should try to carve out time in the daily routine to brainstorm on how to improve the product.

A diverse staff also will bring in a diversity of opinions, and there's nothing wrong with the occasional creative disagreement or debate. Yes-men won't help you succeed and help your business grow. Allow yourself to be challenged without perceiving it as a threat to your authority. I've experimented with all types of strategies in leading teams and coaching staffs, and I can assure you that intimidation is a short-lived and ineffective way of directing. It stifles creativity and takes the roar out of a young lion.

Along those same lines, you cannot be consumed as the head coach with always being the smartest guy in the meeting room. I'm not intimidated by what an assistant might know; if he knows more than I do in a certain area, it can help us. Only a short-sighted leader would shy away from adding a talented worker based on ego.

In that area I have to give Billy Donovan credit again. He made his Florida coaching staff much stronger in 2004 when he hired veteran Larry Shyatt as his virtual defensive coordinator. Larry is 13 years older than Billy and had been a head coach for six years, but Billy didn't feel threatened. He got a guy who fit in seamlessly and helped make Florida's program championship caliber.

That's just one of the ways it's important to examine yourself as a leader. Another: Determine how valuable you really are. If you call in sick, are you missed? Do the "inmates run the asylum" in your absence, or do your assistants pick up the slack? It's helpful to understand your own personality and management style, and to know how others react to it. That will help you in finding the right people to hire. I know, for example, that I need a staff that can match my work ethic and exceed the work ethic of our competition. That's the baseline job requirement with me. If I'm checking references, the reviews on an applicant's work habits must be glowing. I also don't need assistants whose psyches bruise easily—if we do a poor job scouting an opponent, for example, they're going to hear about it. They'll also hear it when they do their jobs well, of course. But if they collapse under criticism, they probably can't work for me.

When looking for assistants, there are three certain types I always shun:

1. **Moody or cynical people who suck the life out of every positive concept.** We spend a huge amount of time in our program working on building self-esteem. My assistants need to be active participants in helping foster that environment. I have a very low tolerance for staff members who detract from that imperative in any way.

2. **Poorly conditioned people.** They would be inca-
   pable of teaching conditioning and discipline if they
   can't keep themselves in shape (this may only be true
   of a sports team that puts such a high priority on conditioning). True fact: I have put two of my assistants at
   Louisville—Scotty Davenport and Marvin Menzies—on strict diet and conditioning regimens until
   they got themselves in the kind of shape that shows
   their commitment to the program cause. Both went
   on to become head coaches, Scotty at Bellarmine University and Marvin at New Mexico State, and both
   have kept the weight off.

3. **Anyone who doesn't understand team ego.** That's
   vital in hiring *and* recruiting. It absolutely must flow
   through your organization, from the top down.

Let me use an example to explain that last point. Trying to
pound that point home to my Celtics team during one tough
stretch, I brought in Bill Russell—the winningest player in NBA
history, and one of the greatest to play the game. While Wilt
Chamberlain was winning all those scoring titles, Bill was winning all those championships. Nobody who ever played the game
can come close to matching his hardware collection.

I wasn't sure Bill would feel comfortable speaking to the team.
He can be extremely giving and genuine, but in some situations
he also can difficult to deal with—especially if you ask him to
sign an autograph. (I think Bill was turned off by people using his
autographs to sell for a profit.) However, Bill gave us his time,
and then some. He gave us a sharp-edged 20 minutes that provided insight into what he's all about. As it turned out, he watches

almost every Celtics game on satellite, and it was evident how important being a Celtic was to him.

When Bill stepped forward to speak to our players, he wasted no time skewering each individual. He referred to them by number, not by name. "Number 8 [Antoine Walker], he's like a lot of guys I played with. He likes to shoot. It's important that the rest of you guys understand that, because that cat's not changing.

"Number 7 [point guard Kenny Anderson], he likes assists. He holds onto the ball to the end, and if you miss the shot, he's not going to be happy because you just cost him an assist.

"Number 34 [Paul Pierce], he's amazing. After he dunks the ball on a breakaway, he can find the camera every time.

"Number 4 [Tony Battie], he's a great shot blocker. He swats the ball out of bounds and yells. Too bad that when he does that, it's still the other team's ball. I always kept the ball inbounds when I blocked someone's shot.

"Number 52 [Vitaly Potapenko], he doesn't trust Americans. Every time he gets a rebound, he holds the ball and waves it around instead of making an outlet pass. He doesn't trust the American scorekeeper to give him credit for the rebound.

"I know you guys think I'm making fun of you and calling you out for your egos. But I'm the most egotistical son of a bitch who ever played. The only thing is, my ego didn't come from any individual statistics. Your ego is about points, rebounds, and assists. My ego came from the final score. My ego is team ego.

"But then again, what do I know? I've only won 11 world championships, back-to-back college championships, 56 college games in a row, and an Olympic gold medal. And that's why I'm Bill Russell and you're not."

It was a very powerful presentation, from someone with the track record to back up every word. We responded by playing some of our best basketball, winning our next couple of games. I only wish the lessons from Bill had stuck with my players forever.

I want to hire people who can connect with their inner Bill Russell—that is, people who take inordinate pride in the welfare of their team. That's any team they're on: the workplace team, the home team, the community team. If I ask a job candidate what role he sees himself fulfilling, a very good answer is, "whatever the team needs." That doesn't mean we'd put that person in a role that wouldn't play to his strengths or help him succeed, but it would indicate a willingness—even an enthusiasm—to be part of something bigger than himself. Everyone craves individual attention and accolades for a job well done. That's human nature—but the people who keep working for a common cause without waiting for applause, those are the people who help teams win.

Beyond seeking certain types of people and avoiding other types, I've found the value in taking risks at hiring time. They have to be educated risks, of course, not reckless, but safe and predictable hires don't always turn into home runs.

There are five coaches who come to mind when thinking about the positive results of risk taking.

The first is Jeff Van Gundy. In 1986, I hired Jeff as a graduate assistant at Providence—that's an entry-level position low on glamour and long on hours. He had been a junior-varsity coach at McQuade Jesuit High School in Rochester, New York, helping his dad. After interviewing Jeff, I realized he probably played the game on a limited basis. He was not overly dynamic in his interview. Still, there was something that struck a chord with me: I could feel an insatiable passion to teach and be totally immersed in basketball.

I hit a home run with that hire. Jeff's home became my office couch, where he slept at night to beat everyone into work. He'd stay there late hours, distributing basketballs to any player who would come by the gym for extra shooting practice. He just about lived there.

In later years I laughed as I sat back and watched Jeff as a successful head coach in the NBA, and now as an astute TV analyst. It's hard to believe that my young graduate assistant went on to serve as head coach of the New York Knicks and wrestle with Alonzo Mourning's ankle in the playoffs, or coach the Houston Rockets into the playoffs as well.

Next is Jim (Obie) O'Brien. Jim was my assistant with the Knicks in the late 1980s—a very sensitive guy who possessed an incredibly high basketball IQ. After that, Jim was head coach at Dayton for a few years, but it ended badly. Although he was a brilliant X-and-O man, recruiting was not his gig. Because of a rash of injuries and players leaving due to graduation, Dayton's talent level dipped, the program struggled, and he was fired. He left bitter about the way he was treated by the media and fans in Dayton.

I wasn't sure I wanted to hire an assistant who was still suffering from those wounds he suffered as a head coach. I also wasn't sure how ready Obie was to return to the grind of being an assistant coach after enjoying the comforts of being a head coach. When you go from having a comp membership at Dayton Country Club to preparing scouting reports again, it can be a tough transition.

But after talking to Obie for three hours, I realized that my old assistant was still one of the best in the game—and hungrier than ever to prove that the Dayton misfortune would not define his coaching career. I am so thankful I made this hire. Without Jim's tireless work and meticulous preparation for every big game, we would not have won the 1996 national championship. He was every bit as big a factor as any of our players.

Third is Billy Donovan, who followed me as a player from Providence to the Knicks. I had a falling out with Knicks general manager Al Bianchi in 1987, in part because of Billy. Al was a good person and easy to get along with, but from a basketball standpoint, we were polar opposites—and that never works. He liked slow-down, half-court basketball, much like the Bad Boy Pistons of that time.

Before Al left on one scouting trip, he told me to release rookie reserve guard Billy Donovan. If we kept him we'd have to pay his contract for the rest of the year—but the Big East tournament was coming to town, and I didn't have the heart to cut a former Big East hero at that time—I couldn't send Cinderella home before midnight. I kept Billy and swallowed the money, further hurting my relationship with Bianchi.

After that year, Billy ended his pursuit of the NBA dream and took off for Wall Street, where I envisioned him heading up a brokerage company down the road. Later, after I had moved on to Kentucky, Billy called me and said, "I'm making great inroads, but this is not for me. I want to be a coach." I was positive this was a mistake of major proportions. Billy was too mild-mannered and meek to test the shark-infested waters of college coaching and recruiting. I told him his personality didn't fit, but he disagreed.

I told him to think about it for 48 hours and call me back, then I checked to see if we could hire a graduate assistant at Kentucky—no salary, just room, board, and books while working toward a master's degree. Billy gave up Wall Street, packed up his car, and headed to Lexington. Early on, I knew the gamble paid off as his demeanor changed in front of me. I watched Billy put a blue-and-white practice jersey on and demonstrate everything I wanted our new players to do in our system—and I watched him develop the bulldog personality it took to recruit at the highest level.

Billy stayed with me five years—a long time in my demanding system—and then moved on to Marshall as a head coach. After two years there, he went to a struggling Florida program, and in less than a decade, he'd delivered the Gators' first-ever basketball national championships—in back-to-back years. I guess coaching suits him after all.

Next is Reggie Theus. I didn't know Reggie very well when he came looking for a job at Louisville. We all knew his stats: He's one of just seven players in NBA history to score 19,000 points and hand out 6,000 assists. We all knew his face: He'd done quite a bit of work as an NBA analyst and had a lead role as Coach Bill Fuller on the immortal show *Hang Time*. So he'd at least played a coach on TV.

He was a heartthrob in his playing days, a pretty boy. But was he an assistant coach? For me? Could I really see him getting into the office at 6:30 A.M., working all day and making recruiting calls to AAU coaches well into the night? I didn't think he'd like that lifestyle.

When I sat down with him at the big summer AAU event in Las Vegas in July 2003, Reggie told me he couldn't catch a break. Nobody, he said, thought he was serious about doing the grunt work, but I checked around. I talked to the coach he worked for one year as a volunteer assistant at Cal State–Los Angeles. He assured me that Reggie had a genuine passion for coaching, and Reggie himself was very convincing. I took a chance.

He wound up being one of our most valuable recruiters and was a key part of our 2005 Final Four team. That taught me another valuable lesson: Form your own opinions, based on thorough research. Reggie was surprisingly passionate and dedicated to the game of basketball. After two years with our program, he became a head coach at New Mexico State and resurrected that program. After two years there, he became the leader of the NBA Sacramento Kings, where he's coming off a solid debut season.

Finally, Walter McCarty: He was one of the true leaders of our national championship team at Kentucky, and he played for me in Boston as well. In fact, I might have taken more grief for giving him a $10 million contract than any coach in NBA history, but that was how much I loved Walt's impact on our franchise. He was the consummate pro, and everything he did was for the group first and himself second—he had team ego—but when it came to coaching, Walter was a complete novice. He'd never done it, anywhere. At least Theus had a tiny bit of experience.

What, beyond loyalty, would make me hire him? I knew Walter's wisdom would impact our players. He'd be a positive influence on their hurried lives as they tried to rush through our microwave culture and into the NBA. He was a four-year collegian who never worried about his own stats, and his NBA background gave him credibility with our young guys. When he talked—especially to some of our less-mature players, they listened.

With your winning team now formed, be generous with your time and knowledge, and care for their families. Try to create a lifestyle beneficial to all.

The first way to do that is to connect with your employees as best you can. Show them you're human. For some CEOs, that isn't easy; they may be great businesspeople but less skilled in social settings, especially when trying to create a light atmosphere with their staff. It can create an awkward dynamic. You don't want to dissolve the chain of command, but neither do you want to make yourself unapproachable.

I've always been a big believer in using humor to break down barriers, some of it sarcastic—I can stick the needle in pretty well. Making people laugh every once in a while reminds everyone that we're not curing cancer here or fighting terrorism; we're working very hard but having fun and trying to maintain perspective. The mood can be pretty serious when things are not going well, but there always is room for a little levity in every day. If there isn't, something is wrong with the leader or wrong with the group dynamics.

I think it's important to get to know the families of your staff. It can help you understand the way they tick at work, and they'll also appreciate it when a leader takes an interest in their spouse and children. A staff picnic, family invited, going into a basketball season or into a busy time in another profession can help morale and enhance bonding. Having an outing where all work talk is banned can be productive as well; it will force everyone to connect on a different level, and undoubtedly to learn more about their colleagues than they ever previously knew.

Every sports team preaches a family atmosphere, in which players and coaches treat each other like brothers, sisters, mothers, fathers, sons, and daughters. Much of the time these are hollow platitudes; things that sound good, especially to a recruit and his parents, without actually being true. One way to make it more than lip service is to literally have family around. Mine is at our basketball complex quite a bit, which can help humanize the workplace. If my assistants see my wife and kids popping in and out of our offices, it can serve as an in-the-flesh reminder that there's more to life than basketball.

# Rick Pitino "Family Tree"

## Boston University

- **Brett Brown**, former player; assistant coach, San Antonio Spurs

- **Bob Brown**, former assistant; former head coach, Boston University

- **Bill Burke**, former assistant; former head coach, Loyola College

- **John Kuester**, former assistant; assistant coach, Orlando Magic

- **Dan Harwood**, former player; head coach, Magruder High School, Rockville, Maryland

## Providence College

- **Herb Sendek**, former assistant; head coach, Arizona State

  ↓

  - **Sean Miller**, head coach, Xavier
  - **Mark Phelps**, head coach, Drake
  - **Archie Miller**, assistant coach, Ohio State

- **Gordon Chiesa**, former assistant; assistant coach, Seattle Supersonics

- **Ralph Willard**, former assistant; head coach, Holy Cross

  ↓

  - **Tom Crean**, head coach, Indiana
  - **Darrin Horn**, head coach, South Carolina
  - **Cypheus Bunton**, assistant coach, South Carolina

- **Jeff Van Gundy**, former assistant; ESPN analyst, former head coach, New York Knicks and Houston Rockets

- **Billy Donovan**, former player; head coach and two-time national title winner at Florida

  ↓

  - **Anthony Grant**, head coach, Virginia Commonwealth
  - **Donnie Jones**, head coach, Marshall

- **Delray Brooks**, former player; former head coach, Texas Pan-American

- **Carlton Screen**, former player; former assistant coach, Florida Atlantic

## New York Knicks

- **Stu Jackson**, NBA executive, former head coach, Wisconsin

## Kentucky

- **Tubby Smith**, former assistant; head coach, Minnesota

  - **Ron Jirsa**, former head coach, Georgia and Marshall
  - **G. G. Smith**, assistant coach, Loyola College
  - **Saul Smith**, assistant coach, Minnesota
  - **Alvin "Pooh" Williams**, assistant coach, Texas A&M
- **Jim O'Brien**, former assistant; head coach, Indiana Pacers
- **Bernadette Locke-Mattox**, former assistant; former head women's coach, Kentucky
- **John Pelphrey**, former player; head coach, Arkansas
- **Travis Ford**, former player; head coach, Oklahoma State
- **Walter McCarty**, former player; assistant coach, Louisville
- **Steve Masiello**, former player; assistant coach, Louisville
- **Rodrick Rhodes**, former player; former assistant coach, Massachusetts and Idaho State
- **Jeff Morrow**, former manager; head coach, Jeffersontown (KY) High School (2006 state title winner)
- **Sean Woods**, former player, head coach, Mississippi Valley State
- **Allen Edwards**, former player, assistant coach, Virginia Commonwealth

## Louisville

- **Mick Cronin**, former assistant; head coach, Cincinnati
- **Reggie Theus**, former assistant; head coach, Sacramento Kings
- **Marvin Menzies**, former assistant; head coach, New Mexico State
- **Scott Davenport**, former assistant; head coach, Bellarmine University
- **Hajj Turner**, former player; assistant coach, Vermont
- **Ellis Myles**, former player; assistant strength coach, Louisville
- **Dan McHale**, former manager, assistant coach, Iona

## Boston Celtics

- **Kevin Willard**, former assistant; head coach, Iona

Another way to connect is by having meaningful conversations with your employees and coworkers about their families. Face it; everyone loves to talk about their kids. Find out about their children, and ask after them. When I greet a friend I haven't seen in a while and that person cares more about my children than about me—asking how they're doing, what they're involved in—that takes on extra meaning. It helps make that relationship deeper than one based solely on the ups and downs of a basketball season.

I want to know my assistants' families. A good example is my current assistant Steve Masiello—he was a ballboy for me as a kid when I coached the Knicks, then he was a walk-on player for me at Kentucky, now he's one of my lead recruiters. Steve is single, so the most important people in his life are his mom and dad. Over the years, they've been incorporated into my family. When my mom was sick with Alzheimer's and lung cancer in New York and I was in Kentucky, Steve Masiello Sr. saw her every Sunday. He'd either go spend time with her or have her driven to their house. That created a familial bond that won't be broken.

Obviously, not every boss-employee relationship is going to be like that, but staff morale is extremely important, so you should search for creative ways to enhance it. I'm not talking grandiose plans as much as small gestures during the dog days of the calendar: Have a meal catered at the office if you're working late; spring for special gear (T-shirts, golf shirts, jackets, etc.) before a major undertaking; leave individual motivational notes on employees' desks; schedule a surprise movie excursion when your team least expects it.

When we have a big victory, it usually is followed by a get-together at my house. I make sure my staff knows they're all welcome—and to bring the wives. That includes trainers, managers, even the police officer who provides locker-room security for us. They're all part of the team effort to be successful.

During my younger days at Kentucky, we'd sometimes stay up until the sunrise after the really big victories. Now we're a little older and need our beauty rest, but we'll definitely still take the time to rejoice. When you spend that much time working to prepare for those games, you want to take the time to celebrate after the work pays off. Hard work makes the end result rewarding, but at the same time the end result must be embraced as well. It's unhealthy to simply move joylessly from one task to the next without stopping to enjoy the successes along the way.

One of the reasons employees don't feel great loyalty to their companies is because they often don't "feel the love" from the company. If you asked the assistants who have worked for me, they'd probably paint a similar picture: It's very intense, the hours are very long, the experience is very unique—but I believe they'd all say they were convinced that everyone in the program has each other's back. We try to foster that kind of unity—and sharing in the spoils of victory is an important inducement to keep the good times coming.

My friend David Novak is the CEO of Yum! Brands, whose holdings include KFC, Taco Bell, Pizza Hut, A&W, and Long John Silver's restaurants. He has made a specific goal of spreading recognition for jobs well done throughout a sprawling corporation that has more than 1 million employees worldwide. Not only that, David tries to have fun doing it—he doesn't just hand out a plaque with a name on it. Among the awards David might present to his employees is a set of chattering teeth on legs, symbolic of the company's goal of "walking the talk" when it comes to customer service. The award also includes a $300 cash prize, and winners can be found from Baltimore to Beijing.

Sharing the wealth can also be a literal means to improving rapport between boss and subordinates. I believe many CEOs would be better served if they distributed a portion of their huge incentive bonus checks among their valuable team members. It builds loyalty and creates an eagerness to work hard and improve the company. If they see that the boss isn't just in it for herself, they won't be, either.

Your trickle-down generosity should result in a trickle-up work ethic and higher office morale. You have to share all rewards gained through victory. You cannot live on an island—but by the same token, you don't want your employees to live on an island. A diligent CEO knows the families—and family dynamics—of his employees, and how those people might affect each employee's performance. It's important for the CEO to develop a personal touch with his workers—lead and also be able to relate, while sharing all successes under the banner of building team ego.

I had an interesting dinner not long ago with Mike Repole, one of the founders of Vitaminwater. He'd started the company while working for Mystic Beverage and moonlighting as an assistant high school basketball coach at Christ the King High School in New York. It was a small start-up company that couldn't afford to pay much, so it gave stock options to employees and endorsers alike, such as New York Met David Wright. The pitch was to grow with the company.

From the mailroom to the custodians to the vice presidents, they handed out stock options as articles of faith in the company's future. Needless to say, when Vitaminwater sold for $4.2 billion to Coca-Cola in 2007, his employees thought he was the Boss of the Year. They had a big celebration after that sale went through. The company had completed its mission statement of helping people reach their professional, personal, and financial goals. No CEO epitomizes making a lifestyle beneficial to all better than Mike Repole.

I also believe it's vitally important to extend your generosity beyond the walls of your company. A good CEO should strive to leave a legacy. If greatness occurs in a one-person vacuum, is it really all that great? Your life's work should send a positive ripple through your family, your business, and your community. You have a chance to change people for the better; don't abdicate that opportunity and responsibility.

I became more outward-oriented after 9/11 and the death of Billy Minardi. It was a proper means of honoring a man who did so much to create and build relationships between others. We used to call Billy "The Connector," because he brought people together from different walks of life and fostered friendships between them.

There is no better example of that than the membership of Old Memorial Golf Club, an exclusive links course in Tampa. It was cofounded by my friend Chris Sullivan, owner of the Outback restaurant chain, but it quickly became populated with friends of Billy's. I introduced Billy to Chris and all his gang, and he introduced them to an array of his friends from Wall Street. Pretty soon, Old Memorial's membership roster was dotted with New York investors and brokers, and I had all these friends I otherwise wouldn't know through Billy. He connected the dots. That was his job on Wall Street—connecting the buy side with the sell side on bonds—and it seamlessly carried over to his personal life.

He'd meet people one time, and a friendship would flourish. It would start with a warm hello and an active interest in getting to know what that person was all about. Then it was a follow-up e-mail or phone call, a round of golf, a dinner. Next thing you know, you'd become close friends with Billy Minardi. He was infectious.

Billy had such an impact on everyone at Old Memorial that after 9/11, they commissioned a bronze statue of Billy and fellow member Tim Coughlin (no relation to the Giants coach) and placed it by the 10th hole. Both were Cantor Fitzgerald employees who were killed in the World Trade Center attacks. It quickly became custom for everyone—golfers, caddies, and workers—who walked by the statue to reach up and high-five Billy's bronze hand on their way to the next hole. It was a gesture of respect and a good-luck ritual. I think that's a very cool thing. Billy would love it.

For the first four years after 9/11, we had an outing at Old Memorial to memorialize Billy and Timmy. At sunset, everyone would take golf carts out to the statue—about 80 of us—and tell stories about the two of them. We'd bring a beer, toast them, say a prayer, and return to the clubhouse as the sun set. It was amazing to see how many people Billy touched with his ability to connect.

As I stated before, realizing basketball's place in the grand scheme made me focus more on ways to help others. I've always kept charitable endeavors high on my priority list, but this seemed like an additional call to do more.

We all have the means—financially or via volunteerism—to make a difference in our community or anywhere in the world. When we do reach out, the rewards are worth it. Sending that message to the future leaders working beneath you helps pass that generosity forward.

## *Surround Yourself with Future Leaders*

**REBOUND RULES:**

✦ **Hire people who stimulate others** and aspire to be great leaders themselves.

✦ **Take risks, but do your homework first.** An educated risk is much better than a shot in the dark.

✦ **Share everything with the people who help you succeed.** Let the spoils of victory trickle down through your organization, and the morale boost will be profound.

**POINTS OF CAUTION:**

✦ **Don't surround yourself with yes-people** who tell you what you want to hear.

✦ **Don't forget the spousal equation.** If you hire someone who comes with an egomaniacal husband or a moody wife, it will have an effect on your worker's productivity. Get to know them, too.

✦ **Don't neglect the motives of everyone you surround yourself with.** Don't just worry about your players' motivation, but your assistants as well. Find out what makes them tick, and what makes them want to work hard.

# Chapter Ten

# What Is Your Net Worth?

**W**HEN I WALKED into the hospital room, I summoned all the enthusiasm and positive energy I had. On the inside my stomach was churning, but this was no time to think about me. It was time to think about the woman I came to see.

She was a lifelong Louisville fan, stricken with terminal cancer. Shortly before the 2006–07 basketball season got underway, her family contacted me and asked me to visit her. The woman eventually would be moved into hospice care for her final days, but before that happened, they wanted to put a smile on her face at a desperate time.

She had the smile—and tears in her eyes—after her daughter brought me into her room and introduced me to her.

"I watch every game," she said.

"That's great," I responded. "We should be good this year, but you get fired up for next year. We're going to be really good then."

I was trying to give her some hope to latch onto, some motivation to think further down the road. My mind was racing in an effort to find just the right thing to say. I felt sadness being there—sadness for the woman and her family. I flashed back to my late mother, and the pain cancer had inflicted on her. I thought of my son, Daniel, small and lifeless on that hospital table two decades earlier.

Going through that tragedy gave me the strength of perspective, and the gift of empathy. When I go into a hospital to see a sick person today, I know nothing can be as bad as that moment with Daniel. These people can speak to me, even if it's only for a short period of time. Daniel could never speak, never could say goodbye to Joanne and me. After enduring that, I can deal with anything. I could certainly deal with this situation, and I could certainly give this woman the attention she deserved.

When I left her bedside, I felt good. Not high-five happy by any means, but satisfied inside. It wasn't just a nice moment for a dying woman; it was a nice moment for me, too. Taking the time for that short visit was 80 percent to help her, but also 20 percent to help the man in the mirror. I could raise my self-esteem not by winning a basketball game or breaking 80 on the golf course, but by making someone's life a little better. That would have a more enduring effect on my self-esteem.

Visiting the terminally ill is the hardest part of my job—especially the children—but the best way to feel great is to help others, in some small way. Turn yourself outward and find grace in the gift of giving. If you have life in perspective, you can't wallow in your own misery when you see people facing bigger obstacles than yourself. It isn't easy to step out of your own everyday crises, large or small. It isn't easy to involve yourself in a painful or trau-

matic situation that might not end well. But many truly worthwhile endeavors aren't easy.

The feeling I had leaving the hospital that day is the feeling
I've gotten every time I've been asked to visit someone fighting a
deadly disease. I am blessed to be in a position in which I could
help at a very difficult moment, bringing a glimmer of happiness
to a woman when she really needed it. Months later, her daughter
sent me a note saying that her mom had passed, but that she really
cherished the time I spent with her. The heartfelt gratitude came
through in that letter.

That is true net worth.

It's not your bank account or stock portfolio. It's not national
championships or Final Fours. It's not awards or plaques. There is
nothing wrong with attaining wealth and passionately pursuing
success, but those things pale in comparison to having the power
to be a positive impact on your family, friends, and community.
That's a legacy with legs.

When I think of someone with an incredible net worth, I
think of Patrick John Hughes. His son, Patrick Henry Hughes,
plays trumpet in the University of Louisville marching band—but
not without his dad's help. He's confined to a wheelchair after
being born with a rare genetic disorder that left him without
eyes, and with arms and legs that do not straighten properly—but
that doesn't mean he can't march. Forty-six-year-old Patrick John
pushes the wheelchair in perfect time and formation with the rest
of the band while 19-year-old Patrick Henry plays. Patrick John
is there for every practice and for every performance. It is a moving sight to behold, seeing the two of them function as one.

That's just the beginning of what these two do together. Patrick John also pushes his son to class every day and helps him

digest the visual lessons from his teachers. He's helped teach Patrick Henry how to play the piano, and now the younger Hughes has performed at the Kennedy Center and has released a CD of 23 songs.

When he isn't devoting his life to his son, Patrick John Hughes works the graveyard shift at UPS, from 11 P.M. to 5 A.M., and gets a few hours' sleep a night. It's the most admirable act of selflessness I've seen in my life, and it has captured the nation's attention. ABC's *Extreme Makeover: Home Edition* honored the Hughes family with a remodeled house in 2007. Patrick Henry and Patrick John have been featured on dozens of news programs, and have made numerous other appearances around the country. In May of 2007, Patrick Henry and his trumpet played the call to the post for 157,000 people at the Kentucky Derby.

There are so many great lessons for us in the Hughes family story. They're not monetarily wealthy, but they certainly are rich in spirit.

I've had a recurring dream in my life in which I've got to present my life's resume to my Maker. In it, I realize very quickly that He's not overly impressed with going to five Final Fours or an undefeated season in the SEC. He's got an entirely different set of criteria for judging my net worth. I don't think He'll judge me favorably or unfavorably for being Catholic, either. The Web site Adherents.com compiles data on worldwide religions. It estimates that there are 22 religions with at least 500,000 followers each. Obviously, all of those people believe their religion is the correct religion, and that the truth will be discovered on Judgment Day.

Personally, I believe it's more important to be religious than to declare a specific religion superior; to have faith without being critical of other faiths. To do good deeds whenever possible, as opposed to morally judging others because you think you have a greater insight into the wishes of the Almighty. Some of our biggest problems in the world today are rooted in religious fanaticism and intolerance of other views. I don't know that there is such thing as a "chosen" faith, so much as there is a chosen way to live. I don't believe God would exclude a Catholic, a Jew, a Buddhist, a Muslim, or a Hindu simply because they chose the wrong doctrine to follow—not if they've lived a good life. The chosen way, it seems to me, has its underpinnings in kindness, generosity, and humility.

It definitely doesn't have its underpinnings in what you own. I own plenty of nice things, and I don't apologize for that. I understand that material things build ego, but don't build pride. Pride comes from other sources. I don't do one-tenth of 1 percent of what some heroic volunteers do for the sick, suffering, and less fortunate, but I can donate my money to charities, I can donate my time to specific causes and individuals in need, and I can use my leadership position to galvanize others to do the same.

So I've become more generous with my time. I sign anything to raise money for charity. I shake hands. I listen to the fans' stories when they approach me. With perspective comes added patience and added wisdom. I know the impression given by a two-minute conversation can be remembered a lifetime, and can cement a fan's perception of me or my players. Besides, it wasn't too long ago that fans in Boston wanted my scalp, not a handshake.

Those hospital visits can end up being the most rewarding part of my job. The coach of the Louisville Cardinals, or the Kentucky Wildcats, is so revered that whoever holds that job has an opportunity to touch people in a profound way. Not just an opportunity, but a responsibility. It's not the same if you're the coach of the Knicks or the Lakers. I couldn't impact as many lives in the pros by being a basketball coach. Those coaches can be very popular and certainly can be called into a hospital to cheer up a sick person as well, but they don't mean as much to their constituencies. The depth of feeling is different.

In Kentucky, you hear stories about people who were buried with autographed memorabilia in their caskets. You hear about cancer patients refusing morphine on game days because it makes them too drowsy to watch or listen. You realize that basketball is so much bigger than a pleasant diversion to many people—and the bigger it is, the bigger my opportunity to affect people's lives for the better. This happens simply by being a basketball coach, and by responding when people reached out.

There are countless examples of prominent people who are worth plenty, but have built their net worth in a more valuable way. The rising level of philanthropy in our society is an encouraging trend. There are many famous role models out there for us to emulate—maybe not in terms of monetary giving, but in terms of commitment to help others.

Look at what billionaires Bill Gates and Warren Buffett are doing with their incredible wealth. In 2000, Gates and his wife, Melinda, created what has become the world's largest transparently operated charitable foundation, the Bill and Melinda Gates Foundation. What started with $120 million became an endowment of $38.7 billion entering 2008, in part because of a massive gift of Berkshire Hathaway stock from Buffett, the world's richest man. Instead of sitting on their fabulous wealth or simply passing it along to their families, Gates and Buffett are helping a staggering list of beneficiaries from this foundation—both globally and in the United Sates. No wonder *Time* named Bill and Melinda Gates two of its People of the Year for 2005.

Look at what Dick Vitale and Mike Krzyzewski have done for

cancer research. They watched Jim Valvano steadily wasting away with cancer, which must have been very difficult given Jimmy V's vibrant personality. Then the two men turned their grief from that situation into energy, lending powerful support to the V Foundation to fight cancer. I have to believe that even with everything Mike has accomplished as a basketball coach and Dick has accomplished as a broadcaster, both believe that what they're doing for cancer research is more important.

Look at what Brad Pitt is doing in New Orleans, helping to rebuild the Lower Ninth Ward that was devastated by Hurricane Katrina. His Make It Right Foundation is working to raise $22.5 million to build 150 homes for families in the area—and Pitt, who has moved to New Orleans, has been a visible and vital member of the rebuilding effort. He's not just lending his name or checkbook to the cause; he's putting in time on the ground.

Look at what my friend Elaine Wynn is doing in Las Vegas. Elaine and her husband, Steve, have become business giants in the desert—but they're carrying it over to charitable endeavors as well. After four decades of involvement in academic issues in Las Vegas, Elaine has an elementary school named after her. According to *Town & Country*, she has helped establish academic standards for Nevada public schools. In 2007, she also was named the chairwoman of Communities in Schools, the nation's largest dropout-prevention organization, with more than 3,400 public schools requesting aid. She's the first woman to head the organization in its 31-year history.

Look at what Andre Agassi also is doing in Las Vegas. He was a brash and seemingly shallow young tennis star, memorably saying "Image is everything" on commercials, but he grew into a tennis elder statesman and has really blossomed off the court in retirement. His charitable endeavors have made a huge impact:

Agassi's foundation has raised tens of millions of dollars for underprivileged youth and the Andre Agassi College Preparatory Academy in Las Vegas, a K–12 charter school for disadvantaged children, is a thriving enterprise.

Look at what so many people are doing to improve living conditions in Africa. Bono, the charismatic singer for U2, was nominated for the Nobel Peace Prize and was named a *Time* Person of the Year for his activist work in Africa. He has become a regular—albeit unconventional—lobbyist in the halls of power in the United States and around the world, campaigning for debt relief for impoverished African nations. From popes to presidents to common people, Bono has engaged anyone willing to listen and willing to help.

For years, actor George Clooney has been an outspoken advocate for the innocent victims of genocide in the Sudan. He has addressed the United Nations on the matter; has made trips to China and Egypt to ask those governments to intervene; and has participated in the making of two films aimed at raising awareness of the crisis in Darfur. He and fellow actor Don Cheadle have been cited for their work by both the U.N. and the Nobel Peace Prize laureates.

Certainly, don't forget another friend, Kentucky fan, and alum Ashley Judd. Ashley has taken on a prominent role with YouthAIDS, traveling to 10 countries on four continents to help stop the spread of that infectious disease. Ashley is a beautiful woman, but she has immersed herself in some of the ugliest places on earth—slums and brothels in desperately poor areas—in an attempt to help. I loved what Ashley told *Town & Country* in a cover story about her activism: "My meditation teacher was talking about how it's natural to want a little status in this life, to have that sense of security and look good to our peers. But ultimately real happiness can come only from seeing what we can pack into the stream of life, what kind of service we can do." That's exactly the point I'm making here about net worth.

All the years of utilizing your PHD to bring out the best in yourself will allow you to arrive at a place from which you then can help others. In the early stages of your life, while moving up the ladder in any organization or profession, everyone is centered on their own progress. When your self-esteem reaches a plateau of contentment, it's now time to aid others in their journeys.

The key to achieving greatness is not so much what you accomplish, but what others accomplish with your assistance. Enhancing somebody else's life through your experience should be a major motivation later in life. We should all strive to leave the world a little better than we entered it, through whatever means are available to us.

However, not every helpful gesture has to be as grand in scope as what Bill Gates and Warren Buffett are trying to do. For one thing, we don't have that kind of money. Giving generously in proportion to what you have—in terms of money and in terms of time—is what matters. Again, the person you're answering to is in the mirror. If you're doing it for public acclaim and pats on the back, you're missing the point.

That's why finding ways to assist those you know on a daily basis can be rewarding, and can start a chain reaction of giving. For example, I got a call from one of my former Kentucky players from the mid-1990s, Jared Prickett. He was selling real estate in Lexington, Kentucky, but he wanted to get into coaching. I was upfront in telling Jared that I didn't have any jobs available for him at Louisville. He'd also been trying to contact his old Kentucky teammate, Travis Ford, who had just gotten the head coaching job at Oklahoma State, but Travis hadn't returned his calls. I explained to Jared that Travis undoubtedly had 15 people calling him looking for jobs, and he didn't want to tell his friend and former teammate no.

So right then and there, I did what I could to help. I phoned one of my former Louisville assistants, Marvin Menzies, now the head coach at New Mexico State. I asked if he had an open graduate assistant job—lowest on the totem pole—that could go to Jared Prickett. He said he probably could make it happen, if his boss, athletic director McKinley Boston, signed off on it. I told Marvin to send him the message that I'd make a gratis speech to a booster group of Boston's choosing in exchange for giving Jared this chance.

In the time it took to make that phone call, I had opened a door for one of my former players to get into the career field of his choice. So often, connections can help a person more than where they attended school, what their grade-point average was, and what they majored in. I have plenty of connections, so I try to use them to help both sides of the equation—the person looking for a job and the person looking to make a hire. Sometimes one call is all it takes, and then you can watch good things spread and multiply like ripples in a pond.

For instance, one call to Marshall University in 1995 helped get Billy Donovan his first head coaching job. From there, Donovan was off to great success at Florida—and that success helped get a head coaching job for one of Billy's assistants and one of my favorite former players, John Pelphrey. Today Pelphrey is the head coach at Arkansas and competing against Billy in the Southeastern Conference. After Pelphrey moved from Florida, Billy helped two other assistants, Anthony Grant and Donnie Jones, both upgrade to their own head coaching jobs: Grant at Virginia Commonwealth and Jones at Marshall—bringing that 1995 phone call full circle, so to speak.

Believe it or not, those pass-it-forward successes help produce a longer-lasting pride than all the victories and championships and great comebacks. I don't remember every detail of our best seasons—and I have a good memory. Sometimes when fans want to reminisce about some obscure events from years past, I have to remind them that this isn't "Stump the Schwab," the ESPN show on which fans attempted to outwit sports trivia expert Howie Schwab.

For instance, I had to consult Joanne to remember everything we did the night after winning the national championship: We took a limousine after midnight with friends into New York City from the arena in East Rutherford, New Jersey; we went to the China Club and got a bite to eat at 5 A.M.; we stayed up all night; and I made an appearance on *Good Morning America*. Then we flew home and pulled the team bus into Rupp Arena for a celebration with our fans.

It was a career highlight, no doubt about it, and I'd much rather have that championship ring than not have it. Still, the euphoria from winning a title had pretty well dissipated by the end of that summer. The satisfaction from helping others should last a lot longer than that—and it has through the Daniel Pitino Foundation.

In September 1992 when I was coaching at Kentucky, I met Father Ed Bradley at a restaurant I used to own in Lexington, Bravo Pitino. Father Bradley was pastor of St. Stephen Cathedral in Owensboro, Kentucky, and he ran a soup kitchen out of the church's basement for the area's poor. He was a former basketball player at St. Paul High School in tiny Leitchfield, Kentucky, and he was a huge UK fan. I invited him to come say a pregame prayer with our team once the season started, and a friendship was born. Father Bradley became a fixture on our bench, home and away.

During that time, Father Bradley told me about his dream of turning that soup kitchen into a full-blown shelter for abused and neglected women and children. I asked him what it would take to make it happen. He told me he could do it if he had the space and that he had his eye on a nearby building that was on the market for $125,000. We quickly formulated a plan and went to work.

We held a fund-raising golf tournament in Owensboro, and I brought my entire Kentucky team with me. You have to understand; the Wildcats are like rock stars in the state, so this was a tremendous draw. It was especially exciting in a place like Owensboro—bedrock Big Blue territory, but a good 3½ hours from Lexington. They don't get to see the players in person very often.

We raised the money without much trouble. Father Bradley bought the building, and the dream came to fruition when it opened in 1995. Father honored me and my contributions by naming it the Daniel Pitino Shelter. Every year, through the Daniel Pitino Foundation, we give about $60,000 to the shelter. Whenever I'm asked to get involved in a business endeavor, I stipulate that 10 percent of the profit goes to the shelter. A few years ago I agreed to put my name on a wine label—Pitino Grigio—in exchange for a portion of the proceeds from every bottle sold going to the cause as well. If you're committed to making something happen, you can find all kinds of creative avenues to finding funding.

The effort has been worth it. Today, the Daniel Pitino Shelter houses up to 100 women and children every night. At times they shelter more by putting cots in the hallways. There is a free medical clinic that serves residents of the shelter and the poor from surrounding areas, some coming from as far as 40 or 50 miles away. Doctors volunteer their time and medical samples to us. We also have a free legal aid clinic, staffed by volunteer attorneys, who can help women dealing with child-custody or divorce issues. Retired teachers donate their time by coming in to read to children or to help them with their homework. And the soup kitchen remains busy every day. It serves about 125 people daily, including nonresidents in need of a hot meal.

The shelter has been so successful that it recently won the No. 1 Agency Award from the center for Housing and Urban Development, which helps fund it. When presented with the award, Father Bradley said he was told that the Daniel Pitino Shelter was "the Hilton of homeless shelters."

I'm incredibly proud of everything Father Bradley has put together in my son's name, and I'm incredibly indebted to all the volunteers who put in the hours to help the residents of the Daniel Pitino Shelter. They truly are doing God's work, assisting those in acute need. As I told them on one visit to the shelter during Volunteer Appreciation Week, "You are my heroes."

Even though I became the coach at Louisville, which is Kentucky's arch rival, it would never damage my relationship with Father Bradley and his good work. He's still a Kentucky fan, but he'll root for me to do well with the Cardinals—and we're still jointly involved with the shelter.

Every year, our family sends a Christmas present to everyone who works at the shelter, and every year, the basketball program brings a busload of shelter residents and volunteers to one of our Louisville home games—usually the Billy Minardi Classic. Before the game I'll meet with them, and we'll take pictures on the court. The kids especially enjoy getting their pictures taken with the Cardinal mascot.

In 2008, I entered my 16th year in the state of Kentucky. People here love to compare the Cardinals and the Wildcats, so I'm always asked which program has been more fun to coach, which place I've enjoyed more. The answer is that both have been great, but they have not been what I've enjoyed most about being here.

I've enjoyed helping fund the Daniel Pitino Shelter, and raising $4 million for the Daniel Pitino Foundation to help needy children. I've enjoyed mentoring the players and assistant coaches who have gone on to affect people in a positive way. Those things happened at both universities; they transcend school colors and competing loyalties. They're far more important than beating Syracuse to win the 1996 national title, coming back to beat LSU in 1994, or coming back to beat West Virginia in 2005.

The comeback stories that can come out of the shelter are what truly matters. That's why I want my legacy in Kentucky to be the good work done there and through the foundation. It will enrich my net worth like nothing else possibly can.

## *What Is Your Net Worth?*

**REBOUND RULES:**

✦ **Real net worth is far more likely to come from what you do for others, as opposed to what you do for yourself.** If all you have to show for your life's work is a lot of money and prestige, you're not worth as much as you think.

✦ **Acts of charity are almost always difficult.** You're dealing with the less fortunate, and sometimes with the diseased and dying. You'll probably see suffering and sadness, but you'll experience true satisfaction from doing those difficult good deeds.

✦ **If you've achieved a position of some prominence and influence, you can exponentially increase your positive impact.** You can stand as an example and an inspiration to others—but you shouldn't be in it just to burnish your public image. There are plenty of small steps for the less rich and less famous to take to help those around them.

**POINTS OF CAUTION:**

✦ **Don't get caught up in might or right.** You're empowered by giving, not acquiring. And casting stones at other religions or beliefs does nothing to enhance your own state of grace.

+ **Don't pass up an opportunity to help those in your immediate circle.** If you can pick up the phone or write an e-mail that will assist a colleague or friend with a job search, do it gladly.

+ **Don't forget the value a single good deed can have on someone desperately in need of it.** An hour of your time or a donation of your money can help more than you realize. A habit of helping can establish your legacy far beyond what you've done for a living.

# Chapter Eleven

# Retire? Hell No, Redefine

**A** **DECADE AGO,** I had the perfect plan. I'd spend seven years coaching the Boston Celtics, move to the front office for three more, then retire to Miami and live happily ever after. I'd be 55 at the time and ready to enjoy slowing down in south Florida, just the way many financially secure Americans do. I'd wake up when I want, exercise, play a round of golf, read a good book in the sunshine, have a nice dinner. Rinse and repeat.

My failure with the Celtics altered the perfect plan, but that's OK. That happens in life—detours arise, and they must be dealt with instead of regretted. That's one of the abiding philosophies of this book: Accept the detour, learn from the unexpected new path you're on, and arrive at your destination with a greater wisdom and enhanced perspective.

For instance, now that I'm past my target age of 55, I realize that my enticing plan for retirement would have lasted about three months—then I'd be going crazy. A life of leisure is not in my immediate game plan. Today I understand how much more I want to do with my life, and how unprepared I am to downshift my passion into neutral. As long as I have my health, I'll be in constant search of stimulation and fresh challenges. We all should be.

Research has shown that mental activity is vital for sustained mental acuity in old age. Basically, it's "use it or lose it" when it comes to brain function. A study by the Albert Einstein College of Medicine in New York of subjects older than age 75 showed a link between mental activity and a reduced rate of senile dementia. As researchers said in the *New England Journal of Medicine*: "Reading, playing board games, playing musical instruments and dancing were associated with a reduced risk of dementia."

That's why walking away to a slow-paced life of leisure isn't right for me yet, not while I still have my passion and my health. The surest way to lose your edge is to take all the stimulation out of your life. You get too comfortable and you get old in a hurry.

So instead of retiring, I redefined myself. Where once the plan called for a great NBA run followed by a life of leisure in Miami, that's all changed. I'm still a coach—a college coach—and I've happily hunkered down in a state that was completely foreign to me when I first came here in 1989. Even after retirement, we plan on keeping Louisville as our permanent residence—something I never could have dreamed of when I left Kentucky the first time.

Joanne enjoyed our time in Lexington more than most people think, but she's an East Coast girl and was happy to get back there when we went to Boston. The fact that she pushed for me to take the job at Louisville and return to Kentucky is one of the most unexpected events of my life. You could have gotten 1–5 odds on that in 1997, yet here we are now.

Why? Because the people are that kind, generous, and open.

My New York friends and many other people have asked me why I like Kentucky so much, and that's what I come back to. You'll find states that are more aesthetically pleasing, that have more racial diversity and more cultural experiences, but I've never experienced people like Kentuckians when it comes to kindness. It's easy to break through and get to know people, as opposed to the layers of mistrust and guardedness you encounter in many bigger cities. In Kentucky, you get right to the heart of the people. They have made us amazingly welcome in what used to be a strange land.

In addition to these changed circumstances, my redefinition took on other forms. I had to make some concessions to age while simultaneously taking advantage of my accumulated wisdom over the years; I've had to be willing to modernize myself to remain viable in a young man's game.

As a result of those changes, I'm now enjoying coaching more today than at any other period of my life—and I didn't have to change jobs to change course. I could redefine without starting over.

For decades, I got by fine on three to four hours of sleep per night. Now I need five to six. I ask my players not to surrender to fatigue in our system, which puts a huge premium on conditioning, but there is a difference between physical and mental fatigue. I noticed that my productivity suffers without that extra hour or two of sleep, so I made that concession to age.

I've been able to compensate for that concession by being more efficient on the job. Michael Jordan's game evolved that way—as his athleticism decreased, his skill level increased and so did his knowledge of the game's nuances. Instead of jumping over or driving around everybody, he became a deadly jump shooter who capitalized on every small opening the defense gave him. That was a very successful redefinition in Michael's final years as a player.

As stated earlier in this book, I've also moved to lower-impact workouts in an effort to keep my body from breaking down. I still demand great physical condition for myself and everyone I'm surrounded by, but there is a smarter way to go about it. If I'm trying to push through the February grind with a bad back or aching knees, it will take away from my focus on coaching. It's another example of using the accrued wisdom of age—and a dash of humility—to head off potential problems.

After 34 years in the coaching business, I have a thorough understanding of what can be delegated and what the CEO must do him- or herself. I know how to handle most crises that crop up during a day, a week, and a season. I know how long it takes to have a productive staff meeting, team meeting, or film session. Just as importantly, I know what not to do from past missteps.

There isn't a great deal of trial-and-error in the job for me anymore; not a lot of unforeseen surprises that can disrupt my plans. That means my accrued experience is making up for that lost step. I guess you can call it wisdom.

At the same time, I cannot simply rely on my stored knowledge if I'm going to have meaningful interaction with my current Louisville players. I can't coach Earl Clark the way I coached Jamal Mashburn. I can't motivate Terrence Williams the way I motivated Billy Donovan. I can't relate to Jerry Smith the way I related to John Pelphrey. Times have changed, technology has changed, and it would be a missed opportunity to redefine myself if I didn't change some things to stay in touch with modern reality.

This year, for example, I became proficient at text messaging. Since I have teenage children and teenage basketball players, I've learned that it's their favorite mode of communication. I could either be left behind or join the 21st century. So I learned the texting lingo and got onboard. Now I'm sending off text messages left and right. LOL.

I've also taken to watching Black Entertainment Television while I work out at lunch time each day. Yes, really—a fifty-something Italian-American coach is trying to stay current with the young African-American culture. It's not exactly *American Bandstand*, but it helps me stay in tune with the lifestyles of my players. This is a way to bridge our age gap, and to help gain their trust and respect. My body will age, but my mind is staying young for as long as it can.

Mack Brown, the Texas football coach, did something similar a few years back, when the Longhorns won the national championship. He downloaded some of his players' favorite hip-hop onto his iPod, just to help him relate. I think it's imperative for any CEO to find out what moves his young workers. They'll appreciate the effort, and you'll probably gain some valuable insight into what makes them tick.

Most young people are more technologically adept than I am, but I'm working to close that gap as well. I'm upgrading my computer skills so that I can remain abreast of news within the Big East Conference and all of college basketball. I'm working with a young entrepreneur to use computer technology as a teaching tool with our players—years ago I wouldn't have taken the time to meet with him, but I'm more willing to sit and listen now, even if it ends up leading to nothing. In this instance, it could lead to something useful.

We're now exploring an intranet system that would allow me to send video clips of specific plays to the players, so they can quickly absorb lessons on what they did well and did not do well in that day's practice. As soon as practice is over, we can break it down on video in all aspects, with a heavy emphasis on execution and effort—those serve as two of our bedrock words. Through our intranet system, we can have those splices sent to the players that evening. It saves us time instead of having to call them in the next day, and it allows them to judge for themselves how they did and where they can improve their performance. I believe it will help us in three ways: (1) it will provide immediate feedback, when the practice remains fresh in their heads; (2) it will ground them in the reality of what they did and did not do, as opposed to tricking themselves into thinking they performed better than they really did; and (3) it will motivate them to improve and give greater effort the next day.

We're also talking with the same entrepreneur about creating a more extensive and sophisticated computer database on each player we recruit. We can input and/or download video high-lights, statistics, national rankings, and our own rankings and evaluations in a single place on each prospect, while also keeping a log of every communication we've had with each young man. The days of stacking videotapes all over the office are dwindling, and this online video helps keep tabs on players who live in other parts of the country. There still is no replacing the value of giving a prospect the in-person eyeball test, but these advances make it easier to see more of everyone we're recruiting.

Simply put, we're trying to stay ahead of the technological curve.

I'm always looking for new challenges outside basketball as well—like writing this book. I enjoy the process of finding a cre-ative outlet for my motivational thoughts. Writing these books hopefully helps you, the reader, but it also helps me put into con-text where I am in my life's journey—what I've learned from the past, what adventures are ahead, and what I can do today to be ready for them.

Redefining yourself can happen in any occupation and any walk of life. My brother-in-law Billy Minardi was forced into just such a redefinition in the year before he died in the 9/11 attacks. For 20 years, Billy had been a very successful bond broker on Wall Street, earning a seven-figure income, but his firm was downsizing due to technological advances that dramatically limited the workforce. To stay in the business he had to become a trader instead of a broker, which meant he had to pass a Series 7 test.

Billy was very upset about having to make this sudden career change in his 40s, but he was determined to make it work. It was either that or he'd be unemployed. He got tutoring for six months, three nights a week, leading up to the Series 7 test. On the day of the exam, Billy felt outdated as he entered a room filled with men nearly half his age.

Midway through a test that took hours to complete, they were given a 60-minute break. While most of the others went out for lunch, Billy found a nearby Catholic church in Manhattan, Our Lady of Victory. He liked the name. Billy went inside and prayed for 45 minutes for help in passing the test.

He wound up passing the exam by a single point.

Tragically, Billy never got to become a trader, because 9/11 hit before he was to start—but in one of the last acts of his life, Billy Minardi proved he could face younger competition and redefine himself. There was only one way to do it: Roll up the sleeves, get back to the fundamentals of hard work, and overwhelm your misgivings with effort and positive energy.

If we're open to new ways of doing things, there is almost no end to the ways we can challenge ourselves and redefine our lives as we go. We need to be ready to break our own mold and the mold of conventional wisdom. We see movies based on the number of stars awarded by critics, and we choose restaurants based on their awards or how they're rated in surveys. It's not bad to use those for guidance, but sometimes we need to trust our own instincts. Life is not guided by MapQuest or GPS; we need to find our own way. I will walk the streets of New York City, where I grew up and still have a residence, looking in the windows of restaurants. I'll try them out based on my own criteria, and that experience will help me. Experimentation and evaluation are two ways to enhance our growth. Add those two "e" words to execution and effort and you have four valuable "Es" to guide your redefinition.

Along the way to new growth, other aspects of your life will change. From style to substance, as you find out what really matters in life. From curiosity to contentment, as you realize that most of life's big questions deserve simple answers. From ambition to satisfaction, as the race toward tomorrow is replaced by an enjoyment of today. From success to significance, as attaining the corner office becomes less important than helping fulfill the dreams of those outside it. What moves you, why it moves you, and for whom you are moved should shift as well; generally, the focus should expand from "me" to "we." In redefining, you're striving to make life more complete.

Despite my current satisfaction level with coaching, I was tempted to hang it up after the 2006–07 season. That was the time I had originally set for retiring when I came to the Celtics, after all, and we were coming off a difficult season. We'd turned it around after a difficult start—when I faced the darkness of doubt at Notre Dame—but the season was very draining.

I gave it consideration because of some of the challenging personalities of players I had to deal with the last couple of years. I had to decide: Was this the norm of the modern-day player, or just the result of some unfortunate gambles on my part as a recruiter? I realized the latter was true. Redefining my recruiting was the answer; retiring was not.

I had to fine-tune our recruiting process so that we could do more research into the background of our prospects. Even with the NCAA limits on contacts you can have with a recruit, we have to do our due diligence on their families, friends, and advisers—everyone who influences their decision making. Beyond that, I want to know how driven the players themselves are to succeed. I'm now demanding a personality inventory on each recruit.

It's the same for business leaders trying to hire the best employees possible. When making those crucial personnel decisions, there's basically no such thing as too much information. That's why the NBA draft changed so much from the late 1980s with the Knicks to the late '90s with the Celtics: Franchises began to understand how important it was to know everything they could about the players they planned to make millionaires.

In 1987, we had draft information on the basketball strengths and weaknesses of every player, plus analysis of how he'd fit into our system. In 1997, we had dossiers on every potential draft pick's life, right down to speeding tickets and parking tickets. Anything there was to find out about a young man, we found out. Every NBA team hired retired FBI agents or police detectives to conduct background checks and scrutinize every aspect of a player's life, positive and negative.

Basically, you conducted a private investigation into every player's background. When you saw a talented player mysteriously slide in the draft, you figured something in those folders was the reason why. That recruiting shift was part of my redefinition; then a series of staff changes helped give me a chance to further redefine myself.

When assistant coaches Kevin Willard and Marvin Menzies got head coaching jobs at Iona and New Mexico State, respectively, I had to hire two new coaches. That's when I tabbed one of my former players, Walter McCarty, and my son, Richard. The result was a very inexperienced staff. That meant a little more hands-on coaching and scouting for me than in recent years, but that was fine. It's important to keep your finger on the pulse of your organization and to maintain your direct contact with the players.

Being more involved in the daily tasks also had its rewards in working with my staff. I could mentor two talented young people I was very close to, and enjoy watching them grow in the profession. They helped reinvigorate me. It's been especially rewarding having Richard on staff. I had a chance to groom one of my sons firsthand and help him develop into a future head coach. I made him earn his stripes on his own, as a graduate assistant at Providence and then as a full-time assistant at Northeastern and Duquesne. We both needed that; he had to see how other coaches run programs, and I didn't need people complaining about nepotism. Richard proved his worth before coming to Louisville.

Now I can help him prosper in the coaching ranks and show him everything I've learned through the years. At the same time he has been driving me like a brand-new car, pushing me harder than any assistant has in years. On every day off from practice, he scheduled me to see a different sophomore or junior recruit. From Seattle to New York, we flew all over watching players. We took red-eyes from the West Coast, talking about the game and the profession. For the first time since my 20s, I didn't have a day off all season, and I enjoyed every exhausting minute of it. I felt rejuvenated having someone so close to me immerse himself in my vocation.

That was a minor redefinition for me. If you want a major redefinition, take a look at Michael Milken, who went from being
the symbol of Wall Street greed in the 1980s to a renowned phi-
lanthropist in this decade.

Milken was known as the "Junk Bond King" who was indicted
by a federal grand jury in 1989 on 98 counts of racketeering and
fraud. He spent nearly two years in prison for his offenses, and his
reputation was trashed. But after getting out of jail and surviving
prostate cancer, Milken ramped up his charitable endeavors and
became a powerful force for positive change in the medical field. In
2004, *Fortune* put him on the cover under the headline, "The Man
Who Changed Medicine." If Michael Milken can become a laud-
able figure, all things are possible. Don't let anyone tell you there
are no second acts in American lives. One of the great things about
the United States is the constant opportunity to redefine ourselves
as life goes on.

The bottom line is this: People are living longer and staying
healthier as they age, so they should also be able to work longer
and do more if they desire it. Don't let age tell you when to retire.
Let your passion—or lack of it—tell you. If you still have it, keep
feeding it.

Why would U.S. Senator John McCain want to redefine himself as president at age 72? Why would he make a second run at
the presidency, after failing to win the Republican nomination in
2000? Why would he want to depart his very stable position in
the Senate in order to subject himself to the physical and mental
rigors of a coast-to-coast national campaign, matching energy
and endurance against younger rivals?

Because that's his passion, and the amount of passion a person
has for a career pursuit cannot always be measured by that person's age. If elected, John McCain will be the oldest first-term

president in United States history, but that hasn't deterred him. Nor should it, if he feels physically capable of doing the job. In May of 2008, he felt spry enough to make an appearance on *Saturday Night Live*, spoofing the long-running Democratic primary battle between Hillary Clinton and Barack Obama. McCain and his political handlers know the *SNL* demographic skews toward the young, and this was a chance for the septuagenarian to redefine himself with that voting bloc.

Why is Larry Brown returning to the NBA at age 68, redefining himself as the new coach of the Charlotte Bobcats? Because he still has something to give to professional basketball, something to add to his incredibly accomplished curriculum vitae. Larry tried stepping out of coaching for a while, taking the last two seasons off to do some work in the Philadelphia 76ers' front office, but he found himself to be as restless at home as I would be right now playing golf in south Florida. He kept showing up at Villanova games and practices, trying to feed his endless appetite for the game. He wasn't ready to retire, so he did the right thing. He redefined instead. Now Larry has come full circle, back in the same state where he began his head coaching career 36 years ago with the ABA Carolina Cougars, setting the stage for a serendipitous final act.

An outward-oriented mindset is an important component of redefining yourself. All the years of utilizing your PHD to bring out the best in yourself will allow you to arrive at a place where you then can help others. In the early stages of your life, while moving up the ladder in any organization or profession, everyone is centered on their own progress. When your self-esteem reaches a plateau of contentment, it's now time to aid others in their journeys. You have the wisdom to provide a roadmap to success.

Toward that end, I've come up with a new twist on a movie

plot to implement in my own life. I recently watched *The Bucket List*, which stars two of our country's greatest actors, Jack Nicholson and Morgan Freeman, as terminally ill cancer patients. It's a predictable plot: They make a list of everything they'd like to do before they kick the bucket, then set out to check them all off in one last hurrah. It's sad at the end, as you might expect, but the point is to get everything we can out of the journey that is life.

A "bucket list" is not a new concept, but the movie struck a chord with me. I decided to come up with a list of things I want to do now, while healthy—but I don't want some self-centered list that includes breaking 80 in golf or running a sub-six-minute mile. I want my children, Michael, Christopher, Richard, Ryan, and Jaclyn, all to participate. I want each of the kids to pick one experience they want to do with me. That will create 10 shared experiences instead of five—one for each of my children, and one for me with each of them—and will hopefully create cherished memories for all of us. My bucket list is coming together as I write this book. I can't wait to see what their wishes will be. I only hope that climbing a mountain isn't on anyone's list.

Involving my children in my bucket list is another way to think of others before thinking of myself. It also falls in line with my developing philosophy as I age.

The key to achieving greatness is not so much what you accomplish, but what others accomplish with your assistance. Enhancing somebody else's life through your experience should be a major motivation in life. We should all strive to leave the world a little better than we entered it, through whatever means are available to us—but before you exit, make your final act something memorable.

## *Retire? Hell No, Redefine*

**REBOUND RULES:**

◆ **Keep yourself mentally and physically fit,** so you can withstand the rigors of competing in a young person's world. Stay up on the latest technology.

◆ **Use your wisdom as a shining light in the dark.** It gets you to places less-experienced people cannot travel.

◆ **Remember the four Es:** execution and effort, experimentation and evaluation.

**POINTS OF CAUTION:**

◆ **Don't extinguish your passion too soon.** If it's still alive, feed it. Reigniting can be more difficult than sustaining it.

◆ **Don't stop learning.** When you think you know it all, you've probably lost your edge and need to retire. Find other passions to keep yourself stimulated.

◆ **Don't lose touch with your people.** Delegate when necessary, but keep a finger on the pulse of your organization.

# Chapter Twelve
# *The Final Act*

**I**'**VE REACHED MY LAST CHAPTER**—of this book and of my basketball career. This book will only last a few more pages. The career? I have no idea when it will end. That's really not even important. It could be a year, could be 15 years, could be somewhere in between. The important thing is that I recognize the end when it happens. Up until that point, I'll prepare to make this final act my best act: my most passionate, most satisfying, most in-the-moment act yet.

Many people envision their final act to be what they do on their way to heaven's doorstep, or the time spent waiting for the inevitable. It's natural that those thoughts come to mind, but that's not what I'm talking about here.

I'm talking about the way we close a career or a major period in our life. Nobody goes on doing something forever, although college football coaches Joe Paterno and Bobby Bowden seem determined to try. Eventually, there must be a realization of when it's time to exit the stage—and hopefully you come to that realization yourself, and not with someone forcing you out well after the right time has come and gone.

How do you know when you're there? Every individual is different. It happens at various stages for people. It varies according to wealth, health, and the level of contentment they've reached. But along the way to a successful final act, you probably will have encountered most or all of the major themes in this book.

You most likely will have wrestled with the darkness of doubt. Your confidence in yourself has been shaken, by failure or some other form of crisis. Your self-esteem shrank. You questioned everything you believed in, at least for a period of time. But if you faced your doubt head on, you rebounded from it and became a better person because of it.

You probably encountered a personal tragedy somewhere along this journey. How you dealt with it and what you learned in the process will have informed and changed who you are. You gained perspective the hard way, but a valuable way.

You might have developed a life philosophy that helped guide you through those tough times—a PHD, if you will. If you stayed true to your passion, if you stayed hungry to improve, if you directed that hunger with the proper drive, you've emerged in the twilight of your career feeling good.

You stood the test of time—which means you survived the microwave culture. You resisted the temptation of the quick fix in favor of a deeper and more lasting success. You did not panic in times of trouble. You stayed the course while others were veering off at the first temptation.

Along the way you chased greatness. Not simply by wishing to be great, but by putting in the arduous hours of practice and discipline it takes to truly be great. You learned the lesson that greatness is far more often earned through hard work than be-

stowed via natural gifts. You checked your progress toward greatness every day.

You maintained focus on what was truly important. You didn't
stray from your strengths or lose your identity as success took
hold. You didn't surrender your work ethic. You didn't view your
breakthrough as an opportunity to slack off. You viewed it as an
opportunity—maybe even an imperative—to get even better.

You also augmented your strengths and identity with a healthy
acceptance of new ideas and concepts. You didn't simply stand pat
when you reached the top. You broke your own model for success
and made it better.

You became a master chemist along the way, learning the
right way to create cohesion within your organization. You realized that one rogue element can ruin the perfect chemistry formula, and you chose your workers wisely based on that threat.
You became adept at handling the problem personalities that
jeopardize team chemistry, and learned what kind of people help
promote better chemistry.

Once you arrived at the mountaintop, you had the self-assurance
to surround yourself with the best and brightest people you could
find. You hired future stars and worked them hard to maximize
their potential and the potential of your business—then you pushed
them out the door when they were ready for bigger jobs, and
hired the next wave of rising stars. You took satisfaction from
helping protégés find their passion in life—a legacy that can be
had in any line of work.

Finally, somewhere late in the game, you chose redefinition
over retirement. You took inventory of yourself and your family,
realized you had more to do and more to give, and shunned the
lure of the easy chair and the empty days. You knew that sitting
idle was a dangerous premise for a high achiever, so you bypassed

it. Instead, you reinvented yourself and found a fresh set of challenges and goals to attack with the same passion you had in your youth.

Along the way to that reinvention, you developed a new definition of net worth. It no longer correlated to your bank account, stock portfolio, or other trappings of monetary success. It became a reflection of how much good you've done for others—in your family, in your circle of friends, in your community, and in the world. You realized that helping others succeed is as rewarding as helping yourself succeed.

All of your stops in this journey have given you precious wisdom. There are great memories from the high points, but also great lessons learned from the low moments. You can't erase those lows—nothing is bringing back my son Daniel or Billy Minardi, and nothing is changing my final record with the Celtics. However, you can grow from them. Often in life, adversity becomes our greatest educator. I believe that's been true in mine.

Armed with a career's worth of wisdom, now it is time to apply that wisdom to your the final act. The valediction to your vocation. The punctuation to end your profession. If you're lucky, you'll know when the time has come.

There have been countless sad final acts, as successful people held on too long to past exploits and went out the wrong way. You don't want to go out like so many boxers have, fighting for dwindling paychecks long after their skills and dignity left them. You don't want to go out like Willie Mays, stumbling after routine fly balls at Shea Stadium. You don't want to go out like Woody Hayes, either; the great Ohio State coach who punched an opposing player in a bowl game and sullied his winning legacy with a disgraceful incident.

There have been many others who got out too soon instead of

staying too long. One of my former players at Kentucky and with the Celtics, Ron Mercer, retired in 2006 at the very young age of 29. Ron went pro after his sophomore year at Kentucky. He was a smart investor who made plenty of money, and after bouncing around with nine NBA teams over eight years, he decided to leave the game in good health. I was worried that he made a premature decision while still in his physical prime.

After sitting out a couple of years, Ron realized that he still had the passion to play, but now he'd lost some of his conditioning and some of the athleticism that helped make him an elite-level talent. If Ron pursues a comeback, he's going to find out that it's much harder to make a roster now than it would have been had he stayed in the game. Your body will not allow you to get back those years that were lost.

Aging expert Ken Dychtwald has said that his research shows that nearly half of Americans are "quite miserable" in their post-retirement lives. Part of that might be because we're living longer; for many people, retirement isn't just a few golden years before we leave the earth, it's a 20-to-30-year revamping of everything they've known. Part of it might be a lack of vision about what those retirement years will be like. If you haven't thought it out and mapped it out—subject to change, of course—you could quickly and easily be bored and disillusioned.

You want the timing to be right and the execution to be perfect for your final act. You want to use all that accumulated wisdom, gained from a life's work, to hit all the high notes and send yourself out right. All the achievements and the lessons learned about what to do and what to shun, and the roads well traveled and the roads best avoided—they should all help direct the final steps of your journey. You simply need to let it happen and experience it. That's why I say that I flat-out don't care how long my final act lasts—trying to predict it or script it takes away from the enjoyment of each moment as it unfolds. As long as I can be productive and I have an ability to influence, motivate, and help others, I'm fulfilling my passion.

If I'm doing this right and being honest with myself, I'll know when it's time to say good-bye to coaching. It would be great if the timing is as perfect as John Wooden's or John Elway's—Wooden retired after winning the 1975 national college basketball championship, and Elway after winning back-to-back Super Bowls in 1998 and '99, but you don't always go out with a trophy in your hands, and that's OK. The important thing is that you go out happy and fulfilled.

So as I'm performing my final act, I intend to fall back upon the great lesson learned from one of my favorite books, *The Precious Present*, written by Spencer Johnson. I've given copies of it to my family and friends, and I read it to every one of my basketball teams. It's an adult storybook that takes about 30 minutes to read and absorb, but it can stay with you for life. The message is quite succinct and very powerful: You're never happier than when you're in the moment, whatever moment that may be.

To recap the book, an old man is rocking on his porch, watching as a young boy plays and does chores. The boy was happy all the time. Eventually, he got to know the old man, and the boy began to learn about the "precious present." "It is a present because it is a gift," the contented man explained. "It is the best present a person can receive because anyone who receives such a present is happy forever."

The boy wondered what such a precious present could be. He asked if it was a magic ring, a flying carpet, or a sunken treasure. Each time, the old man said no. The boy could never figure out what the old man was talking about that could keep him happy forever.

"The richness is rare, indeed, but the wealth of the present comes only from itself," the old man told him.

As the boy grew into a man, he kept trying to find the precious present. The harder he tried, the unhappier he became, and eventually he became sick and miserable. The last time he went back to consult again with the old man, he found that his mentor had died. The man felt alone.

As Spencer Johnson writes: "The unhappy man was now tired of looking for The Precious Present. He had grown so tired of trying that he simply stopped trying. And then, it happened! He didn't know why it happened when it happened. It just . . . happened! He realized that The Precious Present was just that: the present. Not the past; and not the future, but The Precious Present."

The special gift was in him as a young boy, because he enjoyed every minute of every day, regardless of what he was doing. Whatever occupied him at that moment was all that mattered. The precious present is the tense we live in, there for all of us if we choose to embrace it.

If you're living in the past, you're living with regrets or faded glory. It should be cherished and learned from, but not lived in. After one bad loss with the Celtics, I went on a short rant that became famous. I said, "Larry Bird is not walking through that door, fans. Kevin McHale is not walking through that door, and Robert Parish is not walking through that door. And if you expect them to walk through that door, they're going to be gray and old." My point was this: Dwelling on Boston's glory days wasn't going to help the present situation. We needed everyone—the fans and the media—to stop comparing our under-talented team to one of the greatest teams in the history of the game. But then I was guilty of doing the same thing to myself after I resigned from the Celtics: I lived in the past. I beat myself up over my failure, dwelling on every misstep. The past was toxic.

If you're in a rush to reach the future, you're failing to enjoy life as it happens. It should be planned for, but like the past, it should not be lived in. So many college athletes and young professionals try to live in the future; they're so anxious to fast-forward ahead and accumulate wealth. They don't want to learn their craft; they want to arrive. They don't want to savor the moment; they want to rush ahead and acquire what they don't have. What they're missing is the enjoyment of the most carefree days of their lives, where their only responsibilities are to study hard, practice hard, play hard, and enjoy an incredible social life. Once they sprint into the future, they wind up missing the simple life they no longer have.

You have to stay in the present—the precious present—to get the most satisfaction out of every day. When we truly find contentment in our journey is when we understand Spencer Johnson's message. We're afforded a gift from God to enjoy life in a positive and constructive way.

Hurry and worry don't help. Regrets and recriminations don't help. Trying to control the outcome of everything around you doesn't help. Sometimes, you simply have to focus on making the best of everything that's within your grasp.

If you are living and working in the precious present, you're not worrying about the future and where it is leading as you age. The twilight of your career may be upon you, but that doesn't mean you can't have the same passion for it that you had in your 20s. Stirring your passion for the final act—and augmenting it with years of accrued wisdom—is essential to making it a memorable last moment on your professional stage.

The great thing about waking up healthy each day is that we have a choice. A choice to be happy or sad. A choice to be upbeat and ready to go, or a choice to mope about the responsibilities and challenges that await us. We can tackle the difficult chores early and cruise through a productive day, or we can avoid them and spend all our time dreading the hour when we finally have to face those chores.

That is the beauty of wisdom. We get the opportunity as we get older to use it the right way. We can change lives with it. We can truly appreciate where we are right now.

You don't have to live each day as if it's your last, because that isn't always realistic. However, you can greet each morning invigorated and content, because you have the opportunity to make every day a special day.

## The Final Act

**REBOUND RULES:**

✦ Learn from the past and cherish it, but don't live in it.

✦ Plan for the future and look forward to it, but don't live in it.

✦ Enjoy where you are today, the precious present.

**POINTS OF CAUTION:**

✦ **Don't attach an arbitrary date to your final act.** You should know you've arrived at that point when you stop feeling any passion, hunger, or drive, and only then.

✦ **Don't delude yourself into believing that every final act must end with you finishing at an all-time high.** Not everyone goes out on top. Going out happy and fulfilled is more important.

✦ **Don't half-step anything in your final act.** Devote all your energy and wisdom to going out as the best you can be.